Always a Catholic

Always a Catholic

HOW TO KEEP YOUR KIDS IN
THE FAITH FOR LIFE—
AND BRING THEM BACK IF
THEY HAVE STRAYED

Sebastian Walshe, O. Praem.

Published by
Catholic Answers, Inc.
2020 Gillespie Way
El Cajon, California 92020
1-844-239-4952 orders (toll-free)
619-387-7200 contact
619-387-0042 fax
catholic.com

Printed in the United States of America

Cover design by Theodore Schluenderfritz
Interior design by Claudine Mansour Design

978-1-68357-219-0
978-1-68357-220-6 Kindle
978-1-68357-227-5 ePub

Contents

Editor's Preface

Hilaire Belloc once proposed that just as it is good to have loved one woman since childhood, it is good never to have to return to the Faith.

I think we can agree with this without disdaining converts, reverts, or any others who came into the Church only by a long journey or after having strayed from it for a time. The Master knows that some will go to work in the vineyard at dawn, some at noon, and others right before quitting time, and he rewards them all the same. Yet we also believe that the Faith is ordered not only to our eternal salvation but to earthly ends, too. It gives us peace and purpose. It moves us to good corporal works. It makes missionaries, evangelists, catechists, apologists, priests, martyrs, and everyday saints who cooperate with God in this world to spread the gospel and fill the ranks of the kingdom.

So yes, it *is* good to spend our whole lives, without pause, rooted in the grace of our peace-giving, charity-fueling, saint-making religion.

As a father of seven, I can say—along with you, no doubt, and with millions of other Catholic fathers and mothers around the world—that keeping my children thus rooted in Catholicism for life is a priority of the highest order. On occasion, I feel like I'm up to facing that task with calm, steady endurance. For much of the rest of the time—because you know what children are like and what the world is like—it's a white-knuckle ride of terror and all I can do is hang on.

On this our crazy ride of Catholic parenting, Father Sebastian's wise words in these pages give me a steady handhold to grasp. They do for so many reasons, but I'm struck in particular by two.

First, because Fr. Sebastian reminds us that successful Catholic parenting isn't principally a matter of *technique*. The world is full of how-to products touting formulas and systems: for reducing our waistline and increasing our net worth, for limiting our exposure to the IRS and maximizing our chances against the bookmakers. There's also no shortage of Catholic parenting books (along with what we used to call "tapes") promising family harmony if we just say this novena or employ these three magic phrases (plus three to avoid!) or otherwise learn the One Weird Trick.

This is not to say that practical tidbits are entirely absent from this book. But they have their place—and that place is secondary to the *principles* that Fr. Sebastian lays out. For Catholic parenting, like our own daily conversion, is not a technical affair but a task rooted in unchanging truths: about the nature of marriage and of married couples' participation in the creative life of the Trinity; about the way God made human beings and what he destined us for; about the mysterious workings of grace, often long, slow, and unpredictable, in all our hearts.

The assurance that we can focus on the principles, the big things, and take the small things as they come, is of tremendous comfort.

Even more comforting is a second lesson of this book: *God is our children's father.* He has first claim on loving and caring for them. Our human fatherhood and motherhood to our kids is secondary to and dependent on the love he bears them. And so our job is not like a lifelong version of what we do on Sunday morning: getting them clean and dressed, hair slicked and parted, bow neatly tied behind their frock, to present them silent and pious before the altar for divine approval (we hope).

No, rather it is God who prepares them, cleanses them,

bringing to completion in them the work he began. We co-operate with that work in a profound way, responding to the calling God gave us—but it is his work.

This leads to one of those little Christian paradoxes. Because keeping our kids in the Faith is God's work, it is sacred. And so as with all sacred things we are duty-bound to treat it with every ounce of reverence and skill we can summon. God gave us temporal care of little persons with immortal souls meant to share eternal glory with him. He made us priests of a domestic church. It's an awesome honor and responsibility.

Because it's God's work, however, all the love and care and sacrifice we put into our parenting pale infinitely compared with his. We are decidedly the minority owners in God's family business. *He* calls our children; *he* gives the grace of conversion; *he* leads them to drink of the living waters of truth and sanctification; *he* receives the glory when another soul comes home. Our family ties, products of natural generation, will pass away; but God's communion, the product of supernatural generation, is everlasting.

There is tremendous consolation in all that, isn't there? God desires our children's salvation with more fervency than even the most saintly parent could ever muster, and he has more tools at his disposal than the wisest mom or cleverest dad could dream of. *He wants to crown his own work.* And so he calls us to faithfulness in our cooperation with him; to diligence, to trust and hope—but not to perfection. Whether we're striving to keep our children in the Faith (as we ought) or to bring them back to it (as we ought), we can leave the perfecting to him. Thanks be to God.

—Todd Aglialoro

Acknowledgments

I would like to thank the many Catholic families who have been a shining example of living out the Catholic faith. Their words and lives have been foundational for my understanding of Catholic family life. In particular, I want to acknowledge William and Irene Grimm, who showed me what a truly Catholic family looks like and taught a young convert how to embrace my newfound faith.

Take Courage and Have Hope

---　✳

To have children is to take a *risk*.

A child will drag your heart around with him for the rest of your life. If your child gets sick, your heart will endure his sickness. If your child does something that harms him, your heart will anticipate and experience the hurt. And if your child leaves the Catholic faith you taught and handed on to him, your heart will be burdened by anxiety and fear that he will not inherit the blessings that our faith promises—above all, eternal salvation.

Your child will inevitably discover that he has free will, and as much as you would like to control him, you must come to grips with the fact that you cannot. (To be perfectly honest, you don't even control your adult self all the time the way you would like: "For I know that nothing good dwells within me, that is, in my flesh. I can will what is right, but I cannot do it. For I do not do the good I want, but the evil I do not want is what I do" (Rom. 7:18-19).) So there is the risk, too, of bringing into the world someone you must love but who may not love you or himself the way he ought. It is the same risk that God our Father takes every time he creates a new human soul.

In the face of this danger, you can be tempted to run away out of fear. You may be tempted to give up the hard work of parenting or at least not to have any more children. You may be tempted to protect your heart by building a wall around it so that your children can no longer hurt you. Or you may be tempted to pretend that whatever choices your children make are fine, that they're not hurting themselves after all, regardless of what your faith or common sense teaches you.

None of these is a viable solution. The only real solution is *courage and trust*. Courage is that strength of soul that comes from leaning upon God; trust is the firm belief that God loves your children even more than you do and that he will come to their aid. You must not be afraid to be parents: God has given those children to you, and they will never have another father or mother. You must not be afraid to bear the pain of your children's sufferings and mistakes. The Immaculate Heart of the Blessed Virgin Mary is depicted with seven swords because she refused to build a wall around her heart. And the Sacred Heart of Jesus always has a wound in its side. And you must not be afraid to adhere to the truth, even when that truth is inconvenient and causes a strain on the relationship between you and your children. The truth always sets us free, even the painful truths—*especially* the painful truths.

Neither our Catholic faith nor this book promises to free you from pain or the dangers of having children. It does not promise to take away your children's free will. For it is not a guarantee that your child will stay Catholic. You could do everything right and still have a child leave the Faith. After all, Jesus was the perfect teacher and role model, yet he lost one of his apostles. But in these pages I hope to give you sound advice about three things: 1) how to positively encourage your children to love and practice their Catholic faith; 2) how not to unwittingly place obstacles to your children living out or returning to their Catholic faith; and 3) how to find hope during difficult times and persevere as a Catholic parent.

✳

This book has its origin in many years of experience: my own experience as a Catholic and as a priest, and the experiences of countless Catholic families I have encountered and to whom I have ministered.

Many of those families have done an outstanding job in raising their kids—not only managing to keep all their many children in the Faith through a very tumultuous time in the history of the Church, but even to see that continue into the next generation with faithful grandchildren. Others have evinced serious failures in family life, watching their children go astray.

But whether or not their children have remained Catholic, all these parents possess an instinct that their children are supposed to always be Catholic. This instinct arises from the indelible mark that baptism imprints upon the soul of every person baptized in the Catholic faith. Baptism is a new birth from Mother Church, and just as your children are always your children, whether they acknowledge it or not, so too all people born from Mother Church are always children of the Church, whether they acknowledge it or not. The old saying is deeply true: once a Catholic, always a Catholic!

From the many families I have encountered I have learned much about what to do and what not to do, what works and what does not work, and it is my hope to share what I have learned with you. If you are hoping for a quick-fix, how-to book that promises to keep your kids Catholic with one easy trick, I am sorry to disappoint you! Raising children well in the Catholic faith is not easy, and spiritual health is no more a trick than physical health. Both require hard work and vigilance. The road that leads to Christian maturity is long, arduous, and constant.

Nor is raising your kids in the Faith just about your kids. In fact, much of the advice in this book will focus upon the daily things *you* can and should do to ensure that *you* are spiritually healthy; otherwise you will not be able to guide your children to spiritual health or help restore them to it.

All this being said, there *are* some "tricks of the trade" and relatively easy pointers that we can observe in successful Catholic families: pointers and guideposts that will help you steer clear of obstacles that present stumbling blocks to your children's faith. Again, we see the similarity between spiritual health and health; for although it is never quick or easy to build up physical health and strength, there *are* some relatively quick and easy things you can do to avoid physical sickness and injury.

There is, however, one significant difference between physical health and spiritual health: physical health is not contagious, but spiritual health *is*—as contagious as the joy that is a hallmark of it. That is why saints grow like grapes: in bunches! So the greater your spiritual health and joy, the more likely it is that your kids will catch what you have.

With that said, let's begin. It is a beautiful thing you are endeavoring to accomplish in reading this book: the salvation of your children. God is pleased with your desire, and he will bless you in your efforts!

PART ONE

Keeping Your Kids Catholic

CHAPTER 1

Make Happiness the Reason

When it comes down to it, there is only one reason why your children would leave the Catholic faith: because they think staying Catholic won't make them happy. Happiness is the ultimate reason behind all of our choices, but because it is the ultimate reason, we often take it for granted and find ourselves making decisions based upon more limited goods and perspectives. So often do we get caught up in the choices for more limited goods that we often fail to see the forest for the trees: we forget what the ultimate reason is behind all of our choices. Imagine the following dialogue between a parent and a child:

Wise Parent: Why are you studying right now?

Child: Because I want to get a good grade in my class.

Wise Parent: Why do you want good grades?

Child: Because I want to get into a good college.

Wise Parent: And why do you want to get into a good college?

Child: To get a good job.

Wise Parent: And why do you want to get a good job?

Child: To make lots of money.

Wise Parent: And why do you want to make lots of money?

Child: [Feeling a bit of frustration and thinking to himself: *Isn't it obvious why I want to make a lot of money?! Everyone wants a lot of money!*] Why do I want a lot of money?! Because it gives me the freedom to do whatever I want!

Wise Parent: And why do you want to be able to do whatever you want?

Child: Because it will make me happy, okay?!

Wise Parent: Finally, we have reached the ultimate reason: happiness. Everything you do, you do because you want to be happy. But if you found out that making lots of money would *not* make you happy, but rather would make you unhappy, would you still choose to make a lot of money?

Child: I guess not . . . but it *will* make me happy!

Wise Parent: That remains to be seen.

    Whenever we make a concrete choice, we are trying to find happiness in that choice or at least in something that will happen as a result of that choice. The same principle is at work no matter what particular choices the dialogue starts with: it always ends with "I want to be happy." So if your children decide to stay Catholic it will be because they think it will contribute to their happiness; if they decide to leave the Catholic faith, it will be because they are convinced that their happiness depends on it.

Over the course of our lives, our perspectives on happiness change quite dramatically. Ask a three-year-old if he would like a bowl of ice cream or a fully funded college education at the school of his choosing. Three-year-olds will choose the bowl of ice cream . . . every single time. High school seniors (all, right, *most* high school seniors) would not. Our perspective on happiness does not stop changing once we have reached adulthood. Throughout our whole lives, happiness can look like a moving target depending on what is happening: if we are sick, good health seems like happiness; if our marriage is bad, marital harmony seems like happiness; if money is tight, financial security seems like happiness.

One of the signs of a mature spiritual life is a *stable* view of happiness: an understanding of happiness that both corresponds to our experience and remains unmoved in the midst of the vicissitudes of life. Until someone reaches this understanding of happiness, he will be like "a wave of the sea that is driven and tossed about by the wind" (James 1:6). True happiness is what really satisfies the human heart in every circumstance, not just for a time or in this or that circumstance. The greatest good can't be something that comes and goes.

As a parent, you need not only to acquire a mature understanding of happiness, but to learn the art of gradually leading your children to it. After all, this is the same method God uses with us: at first, he showers us with sensible goods, not as if they were the ultimate fulfilment of our desires but rather as signs of his love and fatherly care. As we grow in our spiritual lives and begin to trust and experience his love, God gives us gifts in human relationships and people who appreciate our gifts and talents. Later, God allows us to experience joy in prayer and the practice of the virtues. Finally, through the gifts of the Holy

Spirit and the Beatitudes, God grants us a deep spiritual joy in desiring and possessing him alone.

You must do something similar with your children. You begin with the goods that they can appreciate and experience: sensible pleasures like candy and warm hugs. Next, with copious praise you encourage them to develop their talents and abilities. It is a natural tendency to correct our children for their faults but not praise them enough for their good deeds—including not just their successes but also their efforts and intentions. As my brother used to say to his children: "I want 'A' effort, not an 'A' grade."

Of course, although we should not act as if the goods of this world, such as bodily pleasure or human honor, are the ultimate purpose of human life, they are nonetheless truly good and are meant to lead to something better and more lasting. God would never have given us the goods of this world if they were inherently obstacles to our salvation. God has given them to us as *means* to our salvation, not obstacles to it. We only make earthly goods into obstacles by loving them, contrary to God's intention, as if they were the ultimate good. Therefore, once children have an experience of these lesser goods and through that experience a sense that they are loved and worthy of love, parents need to introduce their children to prayer, gratitude, and self-sacrificial love. Then they are ready to learn to understand that God is to be desired and loved in everything, and everything is to be loved for God's sake.

Gratitude is one of the most essential dispositions a parent should model and instill. St. Bernard once wrote that God finds the grateful soul irresistible, and he showers even greater gifts upon a grateful soul. Everything we have and are is a gift from God, and unless children understand this they will develop a sense of entitlement that inevitably leads to sadness and resentment. The entitled person thinks he deserves everything he gets, and so *nothing* is seen as a gift and *nothing* comes from love. But when someone appreciates that he came into being from nothing and that his life, his body, his mind, his family, his goods, *everything,* is a gift, and receives these as a gift, he experiences the love of the divine Giver. Moreover, he comes to understand that everything he has from God is at the *service* of God, and is meant to lead us and others to salvation; that is, to union with God.

The purpose in following this path is ultimately to mediate for your children an experience of God's love for them. They need to be affirmed so that they have a deep and abiding sense that it is *good that they exist.* Even the small things, like the look of affection and approval in the eyes of their father, the loving and affectionate touch of their mother, are the beginning of their experience of God's love. If this path of gradually discovering true happiness is derailed, or if they are deprived of the kind of happiness appropriate to their age and maturity, your children can feel as if their upbringing and faith have failed them.

There are several ways in which young people might begin to think that the practice of the Catholic faith will make them unhappy.

First, they might come to make negative associations with the Faith. Perhaps they associate the practice of the Faith with problems in their families (this will be considered in chapter 2). They might also associate it with physical or emotional pain (chapter 3). Finally, the lack of an authentic witness to the Faith in their family life—when parents say one thing and do another—can cause children to disbelieve in the teachings of the Church (chapter 4).

Second, they may find the demands of the Faith unbearable: especially when the moral demands of chastity confront them or if they struggle with scrupulosity. To paraphrase Chesterton, they may find Catholicism difficult and leave it untried. Young people might also become discouraged because they experience the practice of the Faith as a bunch of prohibitions: "Thou shalt nots." This often happens when the Faith is presented primarily in terms of avoiding sin and not enough emphasis is placed upon doing good and growing in happiness. We will consider these problems in chapters 5 and 6.

Third, depending on their temperament and the influences they encounter into their teen and college years, they might come to see Catholicism as a cause of injustice: to indigenous peoples, to women, to those with same-sex attraction, etc. The mood of our culture in this time would convict the Church of such injustices. Catholic education (which begins in the home) must make clear that these apparent injustices are an illusion, a lie, and that in reality, true justice can be secured only by fidelity to the teachings of the Church. We will touch on these problems in chapter 7.

Finally, again being deceived by the spirit of the age they may consider the Catholic faith to be irrational, anti-science, contrary to common sense. Here too, proper Catholic education provides a remedy. We will consider these problems in chapters 7 and 8.

In my experience, these are the primary ways in which a young person becomes convinced that the practice of the Catholic faith will make him unhappy.[1] It is important to be aware of these potential obstacles to their faith so that they can be anticipated and avoided. As the proverb goes: an ounce of prevention is worth a pound of cure. So let's tackle these issues one by one.

---

1 There are, of course, the many cases where a Catholic decides to marry a non-Catholic and begins to practice the faith of his or her spouse. But this is usually a symptom, not the cause, of one of the other causes.

CHAPTER 2

Keep Your Own Faith Strong

---

*

No one can give what he does not already have. You cannot give your children a strong and lively faith unless you have a strong and lively faith. The first rule for keeping your kids Catholic is to *be Catholic yourself*: joyfully and firmly Catholic. If you aren't happy being Catholic, you can hardly expect your kids to hope for happiness in the Faith.

One way to manifest that you are happy to be Catholic is to do more than the bare minimum in practicing your faith. The Church requires sacramental confession at least once per year as a bare minimum. But someone who is fervent in his faith, someone who loves the sacrament and derives happiness from it, will be seen in the confession line more often. The Church requires attendance at Mass on Sundays and holy days of obligation as a bare minimum, but someone who loves the Mass might go daily—even ordering his day to do so.[2] If instead

---

2 St. Thomas Aquinas notes that in the early Church, daily Mass was the norm and only later did the Church institute a requirement for Mass at least on Sundays when the fervor of Christians began to wane.

of giving out Holy Communion the priest distributed hundred-dollar bills, churches would be full every day! We manifest what we love by our actions. And there is practically no better way to demonstrate by action that the Faith leads to happiness than by going to daily Mass together as a family.

Your vocation is the primary way in which you practice and live out your faith. So it is not surprising that your marriage[3] should be the most authentic and reliable test of how you are living out and practicing your own faith. In the second chapter of John's Gospel, we read that it was at a wedding banquet that Jesus first revealed his glory and his disciples first began to believe in him. This is not a coincidence. Marriage reveals God. And your children first begin to believe in God's love for them and faithfulness to them through the love and fidelity they see in your marriage. Note that I said *see*—for the love, affection, and joy of your marriage must be *manifest* for children to sense and learn from it. If you are not visibly happy in your marriage, which reflects the happiness of living the Faith, it will be hard for your children to believe that they will find joy in the practice of the Faith themselves.

Presenting a Unified Front

Fathers and mothers affect the faith of their children differently. I once read a statistic from a study done in Switzerland that, though surprising, confirmed my own sense about how parents influence the faith of their children. When both parents are devoutly religious, the study said, the great majority of the time their children grow up to be devoutly religious. That part is not surprising. But if only one is devoutly religious and the other is not, it continued, then the faith of and devotion (or lack thereof) of the *father* has a much greater influence on

---

3 There are also many cases of unmarried parents raising their children in the Catholic faith. I will address this situation in the next section.

the children than that of the mother.[4] I think we tend to take it for granted that since women are often more devout than their husbands, their faith will have a bigger influence on their children. But the truth is that fathers influence their kids' faith more. So husbands and fathers cannot sit back and leave the religious education to their wives. In fact, if anything they ought to be even *more* involved in their children's Catholic formation than their wives.

It rarely happens that both parents are equally devout in the practice of their Catholic faith, and in some cases, the disparity between spouses in this area is quite pronounced. Sometimes one parent is devoutly Catholic while the other doesn't practice or even profess the Faith. Often, the more devout parent, in an effort to protect children from the negative influence of the unbelieving spouse, may warn them not to trust or be like the other parent.

This is a huge mistake. It tells children that the Catholic religion drives a wedge between their parents. No child will want to keep a faith that sets their mom and dad at odds with each other. And our Catholic faith teaches us that the believing spouse must *sanctify* the unbelieving spouse (see 1 Cor. 7:14). So if you are a devout Catholic with an unbelieving or non-observant spouse, do not criticize or belittle him (or her) or draw attention to your differences before your children. Rather, make every effort to show the utmost love, respect, and affection, and to demonstrate before your children the unity with your spouse that marriage signifies. In this way, you will witness Christian truth and love to your spouse *and* show your children that the Catholic faith draws their parents closer together.

---

4 "The demographic characteristics of the linguistic and religious groups in Switzerland" by Werner Haug and Phillipe Warner of the Federal Statistical Office, Neuchatel. It appears in Volume 2 of *Population Studies No. 31*, a book titled *The Demographic Characteristics of National Minorities in Certain European States*, edited by Werner Haug and others, published by the Council of Europe Directorate General III, Social Cohesion, Strasbourg, January 2000.

This means patient sacrifice; and winning over an unbelieving spouse may take years or decades—or may not ever be apparent to us in this life. But the more faithfully you love God through your spouse, the more your spouse will be inclined to see your faith as a good for him.

For Single Parents

In our world today it's a sad but unavoidable reality that many Catholic parents find themselves raising children without a spouse—because of death or divorce, or because they were never married to begin with. This creates all kinds of practical parenting challenges, but, given the importance of the witness of marriage in raising Catholic children, perhaps none greater than in the task of passing on the Faith.

In the modern world where abortion is so accessible and lauded as a means of empowerment, and where there often is pressure for a woman to abort a child conceived outside of marriage, it is a heroic act for a woman to bring her child to birth. God is very pleased with such a sacrifice. If you have been in this circumstance, you should make sure your child knows that it was for love of him that his mother chose life. Although sex outside of marriage is wrong, children are always a blessing no matter when or how they come. Your child should know that, too.

The sacrament of matrimony is meant to be a sacred sign to everybody—including children—of the union between God and man, Christ and the Church. And so just as the perception that the Faith is a wedge between mom and dad can make children unfavorably disposed toward it, so too can the absence of a marital union, or one rent by divorce, negatively affect a child's spiritual development. Ideally, it is best to repair the situation first by marrying or reconciling with the other parent of your children, but certain circumstances may make this impossible or imprudent.

In such a case, you should strive to help your child to appreciate happy, healthy, Catholic marriages among your family members and friends. If at all possible, try to find someone in such a marriage (such as a parent or a sibling or close friend) with a strong faith who can commit to becoming more deeply involved in your child's life and modeling the virtues of being a Catholic father/husband or mother/wife. The earlier in your child's life that you can do this, the better it will be for your child. Young children may not always seem to need both parents, but in fact, the early years are a most important time for their formation.

You can also encourage your children to believe and hope that even if their own parents were not married or are separated, nevertheless they can enter into a happy marriage and give to their own children something they did not have. This leads us to the next consideration: what is the ideal environment for raising children?

Marks of a Strong Christian Family

To get a better idea of what the best soil is for nourishing the faith of children, it is helpful to paint a picture of the ideal Christian family. So what does a flourishing Christian family look like?

Let's answer that first by examining something that might at first look like a sign of an ideal Christian family but is not. A flourishing Christian family does *not* have to be one with no trials or serious difficulties. In fact, many trials—such as financial failure, personal tragedies, accidents, sickness, physical or mental disabilities, and so on—are not only compatible with a flourishing Christian family, they often cause the supernatural character of a flourishing Christian family to shine forth. Certain Christian virtues simply cannot grow to perfection without being tested through trials and obstacles.

Even the Holy Family experienced hardship through

misunderstandings that were unavoidable, such as when St. Joseph did not understand how his wife was with child (Matt. 1:19) or when Jesus' parents did not understand why he had left without telling them (Luke 2:48). These misunderstandings became the occasion of great trust and the love that "believes all things" (1 Cor. 13:7). St. James says simply: "Consider it all joy, my brethren, when you meet various trials" (James 1:2). Having set aside that misconception, what are some marks of a flourishing Christian family?

First Mark: Integrity

A flourishing Christian family is marked, first, by all its members—father, mother and children—being present and active. The family is not divided by divorce, or by strife between the parents or among the children. The family is often present together as a whole on a daily basis. The father or mother do not go off frequently on their own away from the family. The children spend most of their time together, not out with their friends or at functions apart from the rest of the family.

One of the most difficult challenges young people face in the modern world is the expectation that both parents must work to maintain an adequate standard of living. The powers behind these expectations are largely cultural. Against these cultural influences it is often heard that in a traditional Catholic family, dad works while mom stays home. But the truth is that in a traditional Catholic family *both parents* were usually home with their children. For most of human history, life was agrarian in nature and the family lived and worked together on their farm or in some sort of trade that could be done from home.

It was only with the industrial revolution that fathers left home to work, essentially leaving their wives to be single mothers for most of the waking hours of the day. It's no surprise that women, finding this kind of life excessively burdensome, began to look for relief outside the home as well. This led to the "daycare" system, in which children from a very young age are cared for and educated—both morally and academically—outside the home by persons other than their parents.

In many cases, perhaps, this situation is practically unavoidable. Most people can't simply choose to go back to the culture that existed before the industrial revolution. But this should not prevent us from recognizing that it is not best for children to be cared for by persons other than their parents. No one knows or loves children, and naturally seeks their good, more than their parents. Not only that, but it is easy to see that the natural bonds of affection that children bear toward their parents are weakened when their parents are only part-time caregivers. So despite the challenges our culture poses, the principle still stands: parents should order our lives toward family integrity, maximizing the time they spend together with our spouse raising their own children.

So what are some ways to promote and preserve integrity in the modern, post-industrial-revolution family? First of all, it is important to examine honestly what you really need to live on and raise your children. Many of the amenities and comforts that have become expectations in the modern world (especially in wealthy countries like the United States) are not really necessities. They are only cultural expectations. You don't have to keep up with the Joneses; you have to care for your children. You are raising them for heaven, not Harvard. Cutting unnecessary expenses can make it possible to be a better-integrated family.

One of the blessings of the information revolution—accelerated by the recent pandemic—is an increase in opportunities to earn a living wherever you have a phone and a computer. Many companies are becoming comfortable with remote employment, allowing parents to work from home. It may take some extra discipline to work well and productively while under the same roof as your spouse and young children, but more and more families are showing that this is a viable option that strengthens their integrity.

Another step you might take is to cut back on social activities that take you away from your spouse and children. Of course there may be circumstances in which it's impractical to include your family in such activities, but the general principle holds: if you are married, most of your social interactions should be together with your family. It may seem like an impingement upon your freedom, but freedom is really about the ability to do what is best for you and your true happiness. And it serves your vocation, and thus your happiness in this world and the next, to incorporate your family into most of your social activities.

Second Mark: Communion

Communion is when members within the family share one life. Each person knows, loves, is known by, and is loved by all the others. Typically united by ties of blood and generation, in family communion there is a mutual containment of each in each, or of all in all, by love and knowledge. The partaking together of daily activities, such as common meals, exemplifies this unity.

Within a family, the life of the father is in some sense lived by every other member, since the wife and children know and love and enjoy it with him (or sorrow with him). So too the life of the mother is in some sense lived by every other member, and so on. So the family is not only a community, but also a *communion of persons*, since all the members in some sense live the life of the others.

Communion between spouses is also reflected in marital intercourse that is open to the generation of new life. Self-possession and the capacity to take initiative make communion possible, since nothing gives what it does not possess, and communion at its highest level involves giving oneself. For spouses to reflect and signify the mystery of trinitarian communion, their mutual giving must be a giving of the totality of self: "The total physical self-giving [of intercourse] would be a lie if it were not the sign and fruit of total personal self-giving, in which the whole person, including the temporal dimension, is present" (*Familiaris Consortio* 11).

Last of all, communion implies openness and honesty among the members of a family. Spouses should have no secrets from each other—in imitation of Jesus, who said that he called his disciples friends and not servants "for all that I have heard from my Father I have made known to you" (John 15:15). Likewise, parents should be proactive in letting children know that they want to know about their struggles and difficulties, and should make them feel confident in their parent's help. But think twice about preemptively striking with information your child is not yet seeking.[5] Better to make a habit of checking with your children and of asking them questions about what's on their mind. This is especially true in matters pertaining to sexual morality, since the proper forum to learn about bringing new life into the world is within one's own family.

Children on their part should be open with their parents, especially when they find themselves confronted with temptations to sin. In my experience, children want their parents to talk to them about sexual morality when they are ready. In fact, those times when children do show some embarrassment when parents speak to them about sexual morality are often a sign that the children have already heard something from outside the home about these things. If this is the case, you should be sure to console them and assure them that they should always come to you in the future to talk about these matters.

---

5 One friend of mine told me the story about when his young son asked him in the car out of the blue: "Dad, what is sex?" He wondered how his young, homeschooled son had heard about sex, so he decided to simply reply, "It's another word for gender, such as male and female. Why do you ask?" To his surprise, his son responded, "Oh, I was just trying to come up with words based upon the letters of the license plate of that car in front of us!" The moral of the story is, don't be too quick to discuss things that children are not yet interested in knowing!

Third Mark: Order and Harmony

In a flourishing Christian family, there is order and harmony.[6] The love of a husband for his wife leaves no doubt that he exercises his authority for her good, and that he respects her as an equal, not as if she were one of the children. The husband is called to love his wife as Christ loves the Church—Christ who came to serve and who died for love of his bride. A husband must respect her dignity in this regard both as to the matters and manner in which he exercises his authority. Because the wife, as the bearer and principal caretaker of small children, must first of all attend to the internal ordering of the household, typically deference should be given to her decisions and desires regarding matters pertaining to it. Moreover, the husband should restrict the exercise of his authority to those areas which truly pertain to the common good of the marriage and family, not for the sake of his own private advantage.

In response to her husband's love, the wife is called to acknowledge his legitimate authority. This is a very unpopular teaching today, but it is inescapably revealed in Scripture. And the truth is, in spite of the cultural bias against this teaching, a wife will find it easy to accept her husband's authority when she knows that he loves her as himself. For she will be secure that his choices arise from a genuine desire for her good and the good of the family. Her subjection is thus not one of servitude, but one that involves mutual respect and consideration.

When legitimate disagreements occur between spouses, they should discuss it reasonably, and when (as often happens) the wife has the more reasonable position, the husband ought to defer to it. But sometimes even two reasonable persons can

---

6 St. John Chrysostom describes the blessings of an ordered family: "When they are in harmony, the children are well brought up, and the domestics are in good order, and neighbors, and friends, and relations enjoy the fragrance. But if it be otherwise, all is turned upside down, and thrown into confusion" (Homily XX).

be at an impasse, where no agreement can be reached. And in a family, there are only two parents. There is no tie-breaker vote. If the unity of the family is to be assured, it is necessary, when such an impasse takes place, that there be a final authority for making important decisions bearing upon family life. And it is a revealed truth that this authority belongs to the husband (see 1 Cor. 11:3; Eph. 5:23-24; Num. 30:7-17). This is not because the husband is smarter or holier or more dignified than his wife by virtue of his sex. Even in the Holy Family this was emphatically not the case. The reason why authority belongs to the husband is because he is a sacrament of Christ who is head of the Church. As a consequence of this, God guarantees that he will guide the husband's choices by his special providence.[7]

In a family of order and harmony, the children give honor and cheerful obedience to their parents.[8] Children need to be taught the importance of responding with cheerful obedience to their parents' requests right away, the first time. Teaching this requires day-to-day persistence and patience for months or even years, which can be exhausting, but it yields tremendous fruit. Moreover, the love of the parents for their children leaves

---

7 By way of anecdotal support for this thesis, I have personally seen many cases where God works though the husband in an extraordinary manner when the husband and wife have disagreed. In one case, a young woman was having her first child. A few months before she was due, she started to itch, sometimes even on her palms. She mentioned it to her husband without much concern. But the husband was very concerned and began to research the symptoms. He discovered a rare and potentially fatal condition which could have matched her symptoms, but it was so rare that the wife did not want to spend the money or time seeing a doctor about it. But the husband insisted, and his wife was obedient. Sure enough, it was the disease the husband suspected, and she received treatment that probably saved the life of both the mother and child.

8 Pope St. John Paul II identifies a mistaken concept of this order within a family as one of the root causes of disharmony within a family: "Signs are not lacking of a disturbing degradation of some fundamental values: a mistaken theoretical and practical concept of the independence of the spouses in relation to each other; serious misconceptions regarding the relationship of authority between parents and children" (*Familiaris Consortio* 6).

no doubt that they exercise their authority over their children for their good. As a consequence, the family is able to act together as one and work in harmony with one another. Each member of the family prefers the common good of the family to his private interests.

Fourth Mark: Generating New Life

As St. Thomas Aquinas observed, "The good is diffusive of itself."[9] In other words, goodness draws and incorporates others into its own goodness. The happy family will diffuse its own goodness in the same way and will thus reflect more profoundly the *generative* aspect of communion found in God. A happily married couple who live in a communion of love will be generous in bringing new life into the world and communicating their own happiness to their children.[10] Indeed, this communication of goodness and life to the children is the main business of Christian education, for the life of man is primarily the life of the spirit. It is also a sign for the children of God's love for them[11] as well as the love of the Father for the Son in the Trinity.

Today, even among Catholic spouses, it is often presumed that the Church's teaching that every marital act must be open to life is optional or merely an unrealistic "ideal." In reality, the Church's teaching on sexual morality is essential and absolutely realistic—with the help of God's grace.

Note the false caricature of this teaching. The Church does *not* teach that Catholic couples must have as many children as physically possible. In fact, for serious reasons, the Church

---

9 *Summa Theologiae*, I, q.5, a.4.

10 Plato argues for the intrinsic connection between love and procreation: "[Love] is a longing not for the beautiful itself, but for the conception and generation that the beautiful effects" (*Symposium* 206e).

11 "Parental love is called to become for the children the visible sign of the very love of God" (*Familiaris Consortio* 14).

teaches that couples can use periodic abstinence to prevent conception even for significant periods of time. But contraception is something completely different: morally, spiritually, and psychologically. A typical euphemism for contraception is "protection." You need protection against an enemy. So who is your enemy here? Your spouse? Your future children? How does it affect a marital relationship when, at the moment when you are most intimate, you act as if you need protection against an enemy?

We reach a similar insight when we consider that reproduction is the most fundamental of natural inclinations. The power of reproduction is the essential power of all living things. Every human being, every animal, every living thing has a nature that is inclined to reproduce. The ability to reproduce touches us at the most fundamental level, such that any disorder in the use of the reproductive power has harmful consequences in the whole life of a living being. For human beings, moreover, reproduction transcends the purely physical order—since it causes a new human person with an immaterial and immortal soul to come into existence.

Finally, God intends the generative act itself to be a sign of supernatural realities: a sign that the union of the divine and human natures in Christ as well as the union of Christ with the Church are meant to beget new children in faith: "But to all who received him, who believed in his name, he gave power to become children of God" (John 1:12). Contraception denies this supernatural significance, doing violence not only to the intimacy of husband and wife but to the sacramental meaning of the marital act.

Fifth Mark: Striving Beyond the Natural to the Supernatural
The strongest and most proper mark of a flourishing Christian family is that the supernatural goods of family life are preeminent, completing and perfecting the natural goods of family life.

Sometimes we see Catholic families in which the truths of the Faith hold first place in the lives of the parents and children, but in such a way that natural goods are ignored or even looked upon with suspicion. The family attends daily Mass, the children are all perfectly dressed and well-behaved. But there might be a lack of genuine affection between the husband and wife or between the parents and the children. The father or mother might have a drinking problem. Fear, rather than joy, might be the predominant emotion among the children.

In the long run, such a household is more likely to produce animosity toward the Faith, since the children will associate its truths and practices with negative and painful emotions over the lack of natural goods in the family. The goods of nature and of grace both come from the hands of the good God; and grace is meant to build upon and perfect nature, not to supplant or destroy it.

On the other hand, sometimes we find Catholic families in which the natural goods are emphasized while the supernatural goods are marginalized or treated as mere icing on the cake. Prayer and the sacraments are seen as accessories, not necessary elements of a truly happy family life. Given the opportunity to go to Mass together as a family on the one hand or to spend a leisurely breakfast at home on the other; or given the choice of watching a movie together or saying a family rosary together, the choice is rarely for the supernatural good. Such a family prefers to walk by sight, not by faith.

Both the family that disdains natural goods and the family that neglects supernatural goods miss the mark of a truly flourishing Christian family.

This most proper mark of a flourishing Christian family should be evident in all the other marks listed above. The integrity and unity of the family find their primary motive not in natural benefits but in the fact that it is a living witness to the integrity and unity of the Trinity. The communion and openness among the members of the family are lived in a way that reflects the perfect communion among the three Persons. Spouses are aware that their relationship reflects the relationship between Christ and his Church. Parents see clearly in their love for their children a reflection of the Father's love for themselves. The goods that the parents communicate to their children and to others outside their homes are primarily spiritual goods: the truths of the Faith, the love of prayer and the sacraments, a peaceful and joyful spirit, and so on. The entire life of a flourishing Christian family will be suffused with the supernatural—with faith, hope, and charity—in a way that perfects its natural goods.

The family that exhibits these marks will be fertile soil for vocations to consecrated life. Furthermore, the family itself will, in some way, strive to share in the goods attained through the evangelical counsels (poverty, chastity, and obedience). John Paul II said that "the monastic experience constitutes the heart of Christian life, so much so that it can be proposed as a point of reference for all the baptized."[12] Monastic life is essentially a life given wholly and completely to God. It typically takes the form of three vows or promises that dedicate the whole person to God: the vow of *poverty* by which all one's external possessions are given over to God; the vow of *chastity*, by which the goods of the body are given over to God; and the vow of *obedience*, by which the goods of the soul are given over to God.

Though people in the married state of life do not take such vows, in some way they nonetheless find expression in a happy Christian family. Detachment from wealth, and perhaps even times of actual poverty, will arise naturally from a preference for spiritual goods, such as the virtue of generosity. A love for communion with God in prayer will moderate the desires of the flesh for procreation. The desire to serve one another will express itself in humble mutual subordination. And as spouses

---

12 Address of the Holy Father, John Paul II, to the Congregation of the Holy Ghost, May 25, 2002.

advance in age, as the duty of generating and educating children becomes less urgent and necessary, their life together may look more and more like the life of a brother and sister in a religious community, with their common interactions being more and more directly related to the love, service, and praise of God.

Problems in Marriage and Family Life

The ideal happy family I have described above is rarely the actual situation in which couples find themselves. So what are some of the impediments that prevent couples from having a strong, happy marriage, and what are some healing remedies for these impediments?

One of the biggest mistakes couples make in their approach to their marriage is that they think that their spouse is supposed to make them happy. The strong feelings of romantic love that characterize the beginnings of courtship and marriage can be deceptive. It's true that the way you treat one another during this time of your marriage is a kind of standard for the rest of your marriage, but the emotional inclinations that are behind those actions rarely endure more than a few years.

The truth is that God has made you for himself, not for your spouse or any other creature. And so trying to get happiness from your spouse is like squeezing blood out of a turnip. It's not fair to your spouse to expect him or her to make you happy. And such unrealistic expectations will inevitably lead to bitterness, resentment, and even divorce. So don't be so upset if you sense that your spouse doesn't seem to love you for a time. The most important thing is not that your spouse constantly shows the same amount of love for you, but that your spouse loves Jesus. We tend to judge people's goodness or badness based upon whether they love us or not. But that is to make ourselves out to be God!

The biggest role that Christian spouses play in one another's happiness is how they lead one another to Christ, who *is* your happiness. If spouses pray together and help one another grow in their relationship with Jesus, if they are windows to the heart of Jesus, they will be contributing to one another's happiness in the best possible way. And there is no way to do this unless each spouse has an intimate relationship with Christ in prayer.

It is inevitable that the powerful, positive emotions present at the beginning of married life will decrease in intensity. When these emotions fade, it is important not to think that the marriage is failing. To the contrary, only in this way can true love be intensified and the marriage be strengthened. This transitional time in a marriage is a sign of those transitional times of darkness in the soul's relationship with Christ. True love does not look to the advantages that benefit the self, but rather those that benefit the other. So long as there are strong and pleasant emotions within a marriage, there will always be some doubt about whether the spouses are loving one another for the sake of the pleasant emotions or for the sake of the other. When those pleasant emotions are gone or greatly diminished, spouses are able to see more clearly whether their love is pure and truly directed at the good of the other.

A similar transition happens in our relationship with Christ. Jesus speaks about this in a parable from the Gospel of St. Luke:

> And he said to them, "Which of you who has a friend will go to him at midnight and say to him, 'Friend, lend me three loaves; for a friend of mine has arrived on a journey, and I have nothing to set before him'; and he will answer from within, 'Do not bother me; the door is now shut, and my children are with me in bed; I cannot get up and give you anything'? I tell you, though he will not get up and give him anything because he is his friend, yet because of his importunity he will rise and give him whatever he needs. And I tell you, Ask, and it will be given you; seek, and you will

find; knock, and it will be opened to you. For every
one who asks receives, and he who seeks finds, and to
him who knocks it will be opened" (11:5-10).

We can read this parable about perseverance in prayer in a
spiritual sense. For the "friend" within the house is God, our
Father, to whom our prayers are addressed. Jesus says that "he
will go to him at midnight." Midnight is the time when the
sun is exactly on the opposite side of the earth, so it is the time
when light is farthest away. So Jesus says this to signify that this
prayer is being made in the darkest trials of faith, the darkest
times in our lives.

Such dark times also take place in marriage. This darkness
may be caused by evils in our lives: tragedies, sickness or depression, a sense of being unloved. Or it might be a spiritual,
purifying trial of faith in which God permits us to feel lost
and without any reason for our faith. "And he shall answer
from within: 'Do not bother me, the door is now shut.'" The
door seems to be shut to us because the Christian life can
seem impossible to live at times, and we fall short of following
and conforming ourselves to Christ, who is the only way to
the Father.

"I cannot get up and give you anything." These words indicate the feeling of certitude, during these dark times in our
lives, that we are rejected by God. It is as if we hear God saying
to us: *Stop praying!* But this is not the will of God, since he has
commanded us to pray without ceasing (Luke 18:1). But in
spite of all these trials, the Lord solemnly assures us: "I tell you,
though he will not arise and give him anything because he is
his friend, yet because of his importunity, he will arise and give
him whatever he needs."

When we come to pray, we might think that God will answer our prayers only if we are his friend, only if we are in a
state of grace or holy like the saints. But Jesus tells us that is
not true. He tells us that what is more important than charity

in prayer is perseverance; for not all who have charity at some point will receive what they pray for, but all who persevere to the end shall receive it. If God's gifts are bestowed upon us only on account of our goodness, then the gifts we receive will be limited by the amount of our goodness. But if God's gifts are bestowed upon us on account of *his* goodness, then there is no limit to the goods we shall receive from him in prayer. The perseverance of married couples through these difficult times is a sign and witness of the perseverance to which the soul is called in its relationship with the Lord. He who perseveres to the end in marriage and in prayer shall obtain what he seeks.

Healing Wounds in the Family

Most families suffer from one or more of these wounds; what can be done to heal them? The first thing that must be laid down and accepted if these wounds are to be healed within a family is the indispensable need for conversion: ongoing, permanent conversion. Unless the persons within a family are willing to admit their moral faults and to make a firm purpose of amendment, there will be no possibility of healing. In every marriage, the words "I love you" must sooner or later be followed by the words "I'm sorry." Often these become the most important words in a marriage!

Sometimes it happens that some members of a family are willing and able to convert but others are not. In such cases, full communion cannot be restored, and the persons who are willing to convert and do penance must turn to the Lord as their source of comfort and communion. Although it is painful to live in such circumstances, no one can be truly harmed by the moral fault of another. As Plato convincingly argued, only our own moral fault causes us true harm. No evil done to you can make you a bad person; only the evil that you yourself commit.

Spouses must also adopt an attitude of *mercy* over and above a demand for justice. From the time we are children, we must learn that the family is a place where we find mercy before justice, where each member does his duty regardless of whether others are fulfilling theirs. Small children give little or nothing, but receive everything from their parents and siblings. There is no justice here! Spouses, too, must remember that their vows were not conditional. They do not promise to be faithful and to love only if the other is faithful and loves. Nor should spouses "keep score," that is, constantly keep track of the good they have done for their spouse and demand a like return. Nothing destroys a family like the demand for strict justice.

Sometimes it is asked whether we should forgive a family member if he refuses to ask forgiveness or even fails to acknowledge that he has sinned. We should always be ready to forgive, but ultimate forgiveness itself—entering into communion once again with the offending person—is something that requires repentance on the part of the offender. In fact, typically it would not be good for the one who has sinned to be treated as if he had not sinned, since this would result in his failing to convert, which would contribute to his moral harm.

St. Augustine teaches: "If you are ready to forgive, you have already forgiven. Hold yourself to this that you pray: pray for him that he may ask pardon from you, because you know that it is harmful to him if he does not ask, [so] pray for him that he does ask."[13] Sometimes, however, you can prudently judge that offering forgiveness in words or other signs to someone who has not yet acknowledged his guilt is likely to move him to contrition and repentance. In such a case it can be right to offer words and other signs of forgiveness even if the other does not ask for forgiveness.

Very often I have seen cases where two spouses are bitterly

---

13 Homily 211

upset with one another, and each complains that the reason for bitterness is that the other does not love him enough. The most important thing for each of them is being loved by the other, and yet they hate each other: a great irony. For whatever reason, neither is capable of showing love to the other in a way that the other can experience. But the root problem is that they want to be loved more than to love, and this is the secret of misery. For healing to take place, each family member must commit to loving without expecting love in return. Being loved does not make someone a good person, but loving others does make someone a good person. Yet in order to have the strength to begin to love without expecting love in return, we need to experience being loved by God. When his love pours into our hearts, then we will have a sufficient supply to give to others. "We love because he first loved us" (1 John 4:19).

That being said, it typically happens three or four times over the course of a marriage that the needs of the spouses change so dramatically that they can no longer experience being loved in the same way as before. The wife who at first needed romantic attentiveness now needs someone who will listen and help her with the burdens of raising kids. The husband who at first needed physical affirmation now needs emotional affirmation, and so on. So it is not enough to resolve to love your spouse. You must love your spouse *in a way that he can experience* being loved by you. Loving someone in a way he can't experience is just as useless as not loving him at all.

Another step that can be taken to heal corruptions in family life is to draw close to a flourishing Christian family. Just as damaged cells in a body are healed through contact with healthy cells, so also are damaged families healed by contact with healthy families. This is perhaps the most effective way to overcome corruptions in family communion. For example, in a family where no father is present, the children who are missing their father can see the healthy interaction of a father with his children in a flourishing family. This at once enkindles in the children a desire for a healthy relationship with a father and convinces them of the goodness of having such a healthy relationship. Often, in such cases, the father or mother in a healthy family takes on the role of spiritual father or mother for those who lack healthy relationships with their parents. Many a soul has learned how to live a fruitful and faith-filled family life through friendship with a flourishing Christian family.

Another effective way of healing a defective family is by contact with a healthy religious community. Such an affiliation can greatly supplement the assistance that comes from friendship with a healthy family, since it strengthens the focus on living a truly supernatural life. Spending time together with a religious community at its public hours of prayer, attending conferences by knowledgeable priests and religious, and introducing similar practices into one's home (such as praying the Divine Office together) are great sources of strength and spiritual healing. In some cases, it can be beneficial to seek spiritual guidance on a regular basis from a prudent priest or religious.

All of these practices re-orient the soul toward the things of heaven, and allow you to see your trials and troubles from the trusting perspective of God's providence. In short, we can say that communion begets communion. Those who come into contact with the goodness and beauty of true communion are drawn into that goodness and enabled to share in it themselves.

Finally, in order to heal corruptions within the family, it is essential to practice devotion to the Holy Family, as well as to each of its individual members. Devotion to the Sacred Heart in all of its approved forms will be a great consolation and an assurance of divine love for those who suffer from rejection within their own families. Especially to be recommended is devotion to the Immaculate Heart of Mary through the common recitation of the rosary. May the Immaculate Heart of Mary, which was so loved by Jesus and St. Joseph, be a source of unity and healing in all families who are in need of a mother's tender care and love.

Problems in Marriage that Can't be Fixed

Experience teaches that although most problems within marriage and family life can be fixed, this is not true for all problems. Some problems cannot ever be fixed in this life. For example, problems involving certain serious mental illnesses, hardness of heart on the part of one of the spouses, or other problems involving very serious abuse cannot be solved in such a way that the family can once again live together in a communion of love.

In such cases, the first thing that needs to happen is that the members of the family who are capable of practicing their faith must make an act of trust in God that he permits evil only to draw from it a greater good. And the greater the evil, the greater the good that God will bring out from it. But it may not happen that you will see the good that God intends in this life. Some problems are only fixed in the life to come. And so the theological virtue of hope is essential for someone going through serious, unsolvable problems in his family.

The second thing is for them to do what they can to love and forgive. And though there may be no possibility of a restored communion, at least the readiness to forgive is present. For example, if a woman and her children have been abandoned by her husband, she should not teach her children to hate or reject their father. Instead, she should encourage them to pray and sacrifice for him. After all, he helped give them the greatest gift imaginable: their life, and he more than anyone else deserves the help of those to whom he gave the greatest gift. Ultimately, a parent cannot love his children if he does not love his spouse, for children see themselves as coming equally from both parents. If a child sees his mother rejecting his father, then the part of him that is from his father feels rejected by his mother. And so he cannot feel loved by his mother so long as the mother rejects and hates his father. In the child's mind, he can't help but feel and think, *If you really love me so much, how can you not love and be grateful to the person who, together with you, gave me life?*

Another mistake that spouses make when there are serious, unsolvable problems in a marriage is to quickly divorce and seek out a new marriage. They see their marriage as the problem and divorce as the solution. But in reality, marriage is always something good; it is perfective of the human person both at the natural and supernatural level. The real problem is not the marriage but a lack of virtue in one or both of the spouses. And that is the problem that must be addressed. If you had an infected tooth and it hurt to eat, the solution would not be to stop eating, for eating is perfective of human nature and good for you. The real problem is the bad tooth that needs to be fixed.

Similarly, if marriage is not the problem, divorce is not the solution. True, there are times when the abuse is so serious that the spouses must live apart from one another, or even take legal measures to ensure financial support and protect other rights. But living in separate places or even obtaining a civil divorce does not end a marriage. Spouses have an obligation to do what they can to fulfil their marriage vows even if the other spouse becomes unable or unwilling to fulfil his. Marriage vows are not made conditionally. They do not begin with the word *If.*

These hard sayings that come to us from the teaching of Jesus Christ cannot be kept without the assistance of divine grace. Forgiveness of and fidelity to one who is unfaithful are acts of divine, superhuman love. And so those who find themselves in such tragic situations must first and foremost cultivate a deep, prayerful relationship with Christ, the true and only spouse of the soul.

CHAPTER 3

Meet Your Children Where They Are

Raising children to be strong and lasting in the Faith requires teaching, affirming, and disciplining them in ways that suit them best according to their individual characteristics.

As we noted in chapter 1, for instance, the conviction that the Catholic faith will bring happiness must be instilled in children gradually and in an age-appropriate manner. For little children, who are not capable of understanding the kinds of goods that make for true and lasting happiness, we must use language they *can* understand—the language of "ice cream happiness."

Once I went to Disneyland with my brother's family, and after the day was over, my four-year-old niece exclaimed, "That was fun!" So I thought I would test her. I asked, "Is fun the same thing as happiness?" To which she replied, "I think so." My niece was not a very good philosopher, though she has improved her reasoning skills greatly since that conversation!

Small children are capable of experiencing a very limited range of goods: sensible pleasures. These are the very least

among goods, yet nevertheless, these sensible pleasures serve a
very important role in leading children to virtue and authentic
happiness. Plato once said that the art of educating the young
comprises making the good pleasant and the bad painful.[14] So
the way to plant the first seeds that will convince your children that the practice of the Faith will make them happy is by
way of positive associations with practice of the Faith. Here
are some concrete suggestions for this that I have witnessed in
various devout Catholic families:

1) Make sure that your children have positive experiences
   with the reception of the sacraments. In one family I
   know, the father or the mother would personally be
   involved in preparing their child to make their first
   confession. On the day of the first confession, they
   went to church together and after the confession mom
   or dad would give the child a big hug and tell him how
   proud they were. And then they would go out for ice
   cream, just the two of them, and then come home to
   celebrate with the rest of the family. A similar routine
   took place for First Communion. For confirmation,
   since the children were older, the parents took it as a
   starting point to give greater responsibility and freedom for their child. So at every sacrament, the children
   felt affirmed and supported by their family.

2) Make prayer time family time. Children love to be
   together with their family. It gives them a sense of security and identity. If you pray together as a family,
   not only will you be drawing down God's blessings
   upon your entire family, you will also be connecting
   the practice of your faith and the love of your family
   in the minds and hearts of your children. There is no

---

14 See Aristotle's citation in *Nicomachean Ethics*, II, 3 (1104b12-13).

better way to do this than by means of a family rosary. Other forms of prayer include psalms or short devotional prayers. Such prayers can even be said during breakfast or after dinner.

3) Bedtime is a special time for children. Think upon your own memories of your parents putting you to bed. Each day at bedtime, you can express to your children how much you love them and how grateful you are to God that he gave you such wonderful children as gifts. Every night there should be a time for warm hugs, blessings by dad and mom, and prayers of thanksgiving with each child.

4) Another way to build positive associations with a strong Catholic identity in your children is to follow the rhythm of Catholic liturgy at home. The kids should know the saints being celebrated each day and should be told about their lives in order to foster devotion. On major feast days, make sure there are special events for the family (perhaps a nice meal, or a fun outing). During the penitential seasons, perform a family penance together. Obviously, these penances should be adapted to the age and ability of the children, but everyone should do something significant, not merely a token. This has the effect of building a strong sense of identity, much as athletes or soldiers who make sacrifices together build a strong sense of togetherness.

5) Daily catechesis is also very important. This is especially important for the father. At some regular time each day, read the Gospels with your children, and read about the saint of the day. And it is better if you do not merely lecture. You should also ask your children

questions and reward them for correct answers so
they feel involved and take personal responsibility for
knowing their faith. The angels who announced the
resurrection of Jesus always asked questions of the disciples as a way of leading them to better thoughts.

6) Finally, make sure that the family takes at least one
meal together, preferably dinner. This family meal
strengthens family identity and a sense of belonging.
And, of course, no technology at the dinner table: it
is a time for human conversation and interactions, not
distractions. Without forcing things, try to direct the
conversation at mealtime toward topics related to the
practice of the Faith. Let the children ask questions
and offer their own opinions. If they make mistakes,
don't simply correct them but listen to them and try
to indicate what is true in their position and separate
it from what is false.

In all of these practices, it is important to communicate your
love and affirmation to your children through sensible signs
that cause them joy. Affirmation is a particularly important gift
every parent must give to children. It is telling them through
your actions that *it is good that they exist.* To communicate this
effectively to children, parents must have this conviction within
themselves that it is good that their children exist, and they
must outwardly signify this by sensible gestures of affection,
body language, and words.

It can be difficult for a parent who has not felt this affirmation from his own parents to do this spontaneously. We tend
to imitate our parents' way of interacting with us, and if our
parents did not affirm us, we will often unthinkingly repeat
the same mistakes with our own children. In this regard, I offer
three suggestions.

First, do your best to make frequent acts of forgiveness of

your parents. *We will only inherit the faults of our parents that we refuse to forgive.*

Second, think about what you would have liked to receive from your parents, and try to give that to your kids. My father, for example, remembered that his father was very reserved with praise. Once he was elected vice-president of his high school class, and he came home very happy, but his father said to him, "Too bad, son. Who got president?" That unthinking comment wounded my father for the rest of his life. So my father resolved always to show joy at our successes even when they were small.

Finally, examine your own motivations to make sure that you are not seeking to get love or affection from your children. Your focus as a parent should be to give love and affection, not to get it. Parents who seek to get affirmation from their children often become hurt when they do not get what they want, and then they begin to reject their children.

So those are some concrete suggestions for helping your children form positive associations with the practice of their Catholic faith. These associations are ultimately not the reason for being and staying Catholic—the reason to be Catholic is that the Catholic faith is true. Nevertheless, without these positive associations your children may experience negative associations with the Faith that could obscure its truth or impede their desire to practice it.

Know Your Child's Temperament

Another important element in forming positive associations with the practice of the Faith in ways that can be tailored to your individual children involves knowing your child's *temperament*. Each of your children is unique, and part of each child's unique personality is his temperament: the inborn traits that lead to patterns of behavior and reaction.

The temperaments of your children can make a very significant difference in the associations they form, the way they perceive their upbringing, their relationships with their family, and their interactions with their friends. The same event, words, or actions can be perceived by two children in a radically different way depending upon their temperament. There is an old adage that goes, "Everything is received in the way the receiver is disposed to receive it."

I know some families in which two children raised by the same parents in the same way expressed very different memories of their childhood. Their temperament was like a filter that selected some memories in favor of others to paint a very different experience of their past. Some things that might be no big deal to one child might end up being very significant to another child. For example, if a child is disposed toward melancholy, he might perceive a sharp correction from his parents as extremely emotionally painful, and because of this come to deeply feel that his parents have rejected him; whereas the sting of the very same correction given to a child with a sanguine temperament might be forgotten a few minutes later.

Let's look at a few tips on how to manage children with different temperaments.

The Four Classical Temperaments

The identification of four temperaments—choleric, melancholic, sanguine, and phlegmatic—goes back to ancient sources such as Hippocrates and Galen and was taken up again and developed in the Middle Ages. The enduring character of this doctrine reveals that it has struck on something perennially rooted in human nature. Most people have a predominant temperament (even if they have a secondary temperament and indeed some elements of all four) that has a predominant emotion associated with it as well as a predominant way of responding emotionally to the actions of others and other external events.

In the following descriptions, I will focus upon the strengths and weaknesses of each temperament, but especially upon the weaknesses, since that is where parents have to be especially careful in their upbringing.

The person with a *choleric* temperament is most easily disposed toward anger. When faced with obstacles to their desires, the instinctive emotional response of cholerics is to fight and overcome those obstacles. They can be very hopeful or daring in the face of these obstacles. Because they are often very driven to achieve goals, choleric persons tend to make good leaders, but they also tend to be thoughtless about the effects of their actions upon others.

Cholerics tend to get energy from being around groups of people, and their overall emotional tendency is toward excess. They can easily fly off the handle, but they can also calm down relatively quickly. As children, cholerics tend to get in a lot of trouble because of fighting or not thinking about the needs of others. On the other hand, they are not easily persuaded to follow the crowd, since they don't give in as easily to peer pressure.

The person with the *melancholic* temperament is most easily disposed toward sadness. When faced with significant obstacles to his desires, the instinctive emotional response of the melancholic is to withdraw. Because they feel their emotions very deeply, melancholics tend to be compassionate and thoughtful. They make very faithful friends. But they also get easily discouraged.

Melancholics often feel drained in social settings. Because they hold things inside and are not inclined to share their feelings, they sometimes will ruminate over a past injury and eventually explode in resentment or anger. As children, melancholics tend to be thoughtful of others, obedient, and the source of little trouble, but they also tend to perceive injustices in the way they are treated relative to other children—even if the parent has been treating everyone the same. When this happens, the melancholic child can become peevish and sulk for a long time.

The person with the *sanguine* temperament is most easily
disposed toward joy and desire. When faced with obstacles to
their desires, the sanguine's instinctive emotional response is to
redirect his desires to something else easy and pleasant, or at
least to find some covert way around the obstacle to get what
he wants. Although sanguines are most easily disposed toward
joy, their emotions can fluctuate quite quickly, and they can go
from being very joyful to very sad in a short time, and vice-
versa.

Sanguines make friends easily, and tend to be fun, expressive,
and the life of the party. Like cholerics, they derive energy from
social settings. But their friendships often lack depth, and they
easily move on from one group of friends to another. Also in
similar fashion to cholerics, sanguines tend toward emotional
excess. As children, sanguines often get into trouble for seeking
pleasure, and they often get distracted from schoolwork. They
tend to get over corrections quickly, even harsh ones: so much
so that they sometimes seem to forget that they were ever corrected.

The person with the *phlegmatic* temperament is most easily
disposed toward fear, but not just any fear: fear of hard work or
effort. When faced with obstacles to their desires, the instinctive emotional response of phlegmatics is to give up and stop
caring. For this reason, they sometimes seem to be lacking any
strong emotions. They prefer to be in the background in social
settings, and let others take the lead. They tend to be easygoing,
and good listeners. As such they often make good companions
for people with choleric temperaments.

Phlegmatics' primary weakness is a lack of drive: they too
easily settle for lesser goods and accomplishments. They tend
toward being less emotionally invested than they should be.
But once they make up their mind to do something, they can
be very methodical and persevering. As children, phlegmatics
tend to be well-behaved, but they also need constant prodding
to accomplish their duties. When they are corrected, they tend

to respond dispassionately, taking the correction like water off a duck's back. Often, they put up little resistance to peer pressure, since they tend to take the path of least resistance.

Temperament-Specific Advice

Although knowing the temperament of a person can be helpful in interacting with both adults and children, the advice in this section and the next is primarily geared toward helping parents understand and form their children before they reach their adult years.

With the choleric and sanguine child, the general strategy should be to rein in excessive tendencies. Cholerics and sanguines require frequent and firm correction to moderate their emotional inclinations. At the same time, they should be given opportunities to direct their inclinations toward legitimate and healthy goals. The choleric child should especially be trained to think about the needs of others. The sanguine child should be trained to overcome distractions and to do the good things that are sometimes unpleasant for them. Sanguine children are especially vulnerable to unhealthy romantic relationships when they enter their teenage years. So, much vigilance should be exercised in that regard.

With melancholic and phlegmatic children, the general strategy should be to encourage them to strive for more than they think they can accomplish. When correcting a melancholic child, the parent should be prepared to take some time sitting down with the child, asking why he did certain things and encouraging him to make his feelings known. Melancholics often have a hard time believing that others understand the depth of their sadness or difficulties, and so they need to be assured by their parents that they are understood. Phlegmatic children should also be frequently encouraged and trained to apply themselves consistently and methodically to long-term goals and projects.

Let's go back to Plato's advice for child-rearing: making the good pleasant and the bad painful. In general, positive reinforcement focusing on rewards for good behavior should be the first approach used by parents. But for the choleric and the sanguine, you should be a bit more willing to make use of punishments that make the bad painful, whereas for the melancholic and the phlegmatic the emphasis should lean more toward rewards that make the good pleasant.

Children's Temperaments and the Practice of the Faith

Your child's temperament also has a bearing upon specific aspects of the practice of the Faith. Understanding this can help you more capably form your children in these areas.

Prayer

Prayer requires patience and sometimes long periods of silence and stillness. And if it is private prayer, it may also involve remaining alone for significant amounts of time. For this reason, those with a melancholic temperament, who like long, quiet times alone, tend to enjoy prayer more than those with other temperaments. As introverts, they feel drained in social situations and recharged when they are alone and not under any pressure or expectations regarding others. The pitfall the melancholic needs to avoid is turning prayer into self-serving emotional consolation, rather than time devoted to conversation with the Lord and making good resolutions.

Those with an extroverted sanguine temperament, on the other hand, often suffer from distractions during times of prayer. They tend to fidget and want to do something that involves more social interaction or external stimuli. Your sanguine children will need to be trained gradually to lengthen their time of private prayer and to focus on Christ during prayer. Cholerics also tend to suffer from distractions during prayer, especially if they have been offended or resisted recently by someone. They can also embrace prayer rather intensely because they see it as a means of obtaining their desires. A choleric needs to be trained to love prayer for its own sake and to spend time in prayer as a way of calming anger and offering forgiveness.

Finally, the phlegmatic, like the melancholic, tends to find the quiet and solitude of prayer easy and natural. So much so, however, that the phlegmatic often tends to "zone out" or even fall asleep during prayer. For phlegmatics, the pitfall of prayer is that it becomes an opportunity for laziness rather than an opportunity for deepening their relationship with Christ. So your phlegmatic child should be trained to put effort and focus into their prayer. It is especially profitable for a phlegmatic to employ good spiritual reading together with prayer as a means of staying focused and alert.

Perseverance in Prayer and Good Deeds

Another area where temperament can influence the practice of the Faith is in perseverance in prayer and good works. Children, in general, struggle to persevere in their good intentions. They may try to commit themselves to daily prayer (such as the rosary) but only make it a few days before they give up; or they pledge to make it to confession every month but soon start to skip months. Among the four temperaments, melancholics and cholerics tend to persevere best. It is more difficult for phlegmatics and sanguines to persevere well.

The key for melancholics and cholerics is to convince them that they should care about prayer. Once a child with a melancholic or choleric temperament experiences the benefits of prayer and begins to be personally invested in prayer, his temperament will naturally assist him in persevering. However, what makes a child care and become personally invested differs from individual to individual, even among children with the same temperament. For example, if a particular child loves to hear stories about the lives of the saints, then pointing out that prayer is the only path to becoming a saint would be likely to generate interest in him. Another child, though, may really enjoy one-on-one time with a parent, so for him a visit to a holy hour or other prayer time with you might be what kindles and holds his interest.

The sanguine and phlegmatic child also need to become personally invested in prayer in order to persevere. But they will need regular encouragement and enticements as well. Sanguines, for example, may get bored easily because of the many distractions they encounter in their imagination while they pray. A phlegmatic might have a hard time motivating himself to put forth the effort involved in prayer. In these cases, it is always helpful to give words of praise and encouragement as well as pleasant rewards for persevering in prayer.

For example, telling your child how much you respect his effort in persevering, and how proud you are of him for not giving up, gives your child motivation to continue his efforts. And if you see him slacking in his commitments, instead of being critical or disappointed you could offer to help him stay firm. Another effective enticement could be hosting a gathering of your children's friends as a reward for persevering prayer. You could even juxtapose the two events: a holy hour with friends followed by a social gathering. Church youth groups that include regular prayer as part of their activities are also extremely helpful in strengthening a young person's resolve to persevere in prayer. And the same kinds of things that encourage perseverance in prayer will also help encourage perseverance in good works.

The Sacraments
The principal sacraments that need to be frequented regularly are confession and the Eucharist. As a rule of thumb, confession

should be frequented once a month[15] (or if needed, more frequently). Ideally, Mass and Holy Communion should be encouraged daily, but at the very least weekly.

By frequent attendance at Mass and reception of the Eucharist I mean more often than on Sundays and holy days of obligation (for example, daily Mass or Mass on certain days during the week). Perseverance in frequent Mass and Communion comes along with perseverance in prayer, so the temperament-specific advice I gave about prayer above is applicable also for Mass and the reception of Holy Communion.

A parent must be very delicate in encouraging regular Communion. St. Thomas Aquinas points out that the ideal frequency of Communion should be determined by the degree of devotion in an individual's soul. If once-a-week reception brings about the greatest devotion for a person, then that would be the ideal for him. If reception once a day brings about the greatest devotion, then that would be ideal. One mistake parents often make is to watch carefully to see if their children are receiving the Eucharist, and then asking probing questions or assuming that they are in mortal sin if their child did not receive on a given day. Pressure like this from a parent may have the unintended effect of encouraging sacrilegious Communions or at least devotionless Communions. A child becomes fearful that his parents will be angry or disappointed, so he receives Communion even if he is not properly disposed.

Instead of asking probing questions, the main thing you can do is make it easy for your children to get to confession regularly. If your child is going to confession regularly, then it is likely that he will overcome the obstacles that prevent him from

---

15 This frequency is implied in the Church's usage for granting plenary indulgences, since if someone goes to confession every four weeks, he will always fulfill the condition of going to confession two weeks before or after the indulgenced work.

receiving Holy Communion and that when he does receive Communion, that he will be properly disposed. Meanwhile, if anything, you should feel (and express) satisfaction when your child chooses to abstain from Communion on occasion. This shows that he is not acting out of human respect but out of a sincere desire to receive the Eucharist well.

The desire of a child to make a regular confession can be influenced by his temperament in particular ways. If you have a melancholic child, it is beneficial to find a priest who is gentle and kind in the confessional. A melancholic can have one bad experience in the confessional with a harsh priest and be scared to return to confession for a long time. Phlegmatics and sanguines tend to have a hard time motivating themselves to go to confession, so in their cases it can be an enticement to make going to confession an opportunity for one-on-one time with dad or mom, or perhaps arrange a group (either of family or friends) to make going to confession more of a social event. Finally, cholerics need to be convinced of the great benefits of confession. Once a choleric sees the utility of confession, he will usually be good at making regular use of the sacrament on his own initiative.

CHAPTER 4

Seek First the Kingdom of God

--- ✳ ---

Once I was taking a group of high school students to visit Thomas Aquinas College to see if they might be interested in attending. Many of them had concerns about whether they could get high-paying jobs after graduation, so I had them meet with the founding president of the college, Ron MacArthur.

I thought that he would give them some explanation about how we are all seeking happiness, how money is only instrumental in removing certain obstacles to happiness, not providing happiness, and how alumni of the college had a zero-percent default rate on their student loans, showing that all the graduates were capable of providing for themselves and their sizable families. But instead of saying all that, he said something that surprised me and has always stayed with me. He said to the students, "Well, that attitude just isn't Christian. We are told to seek first the kingdom of God, not financial success. You just aren't following the gospel if you think that you should pursue an education for the primary reason of getting a high-paying job."

That fundamental disposition toward life—of trusting God to take care of your basic human needs—is something that is becoming rarer and rarer in the Christian West. We have become so used to providing for ourselves that we rarely, if ever, have to seriously pray, "Give us this day our daily bread."

Children are not stupid. They can figure out if material prosperity is more important to you than the practice of their faith. They can also tell if you think that material prosperity is part of what you think Christ promises: the "health and wealth gospel." Passages in Scripture such as the Beatitudes' "Blessed are the poor" are very difficult to reconcile with the actual lives of their parents who are making great efforts to live in prosperity. Now this is a hard saying. But if your actions teach your children that material prosperity is essential to the living out of your faith, you might as well tell your kids to leave the Church now. No one can remain authentically Catholic who cannot trust in the providence of their Father in heaven.

The Dangers of Wealth

Here it is appropriate to consider the teachings of Jesus about the dangers of wealth. According to the Gospel of St. Luke, Jesus said, "How hard it is for those who have riches to enter the kingdom of God!" (18:24). In the next verse he added that it is harder for a rich man to enter the kingdom of heaven than for a camel to pass through the eye of a needle. If the Lord had given such dire warnings about anything else, I suppose not one Christian in the world would seek that thing. But since the human heart so desperately clings to wealth, there are many Christians who make every excuse to seek to be wealthy. This should give us pause.

Scripture points out three dangers of wealth. The first is to those who are so attached to wealth that they are willing to commit injustice in order to gain or keep their wealth. Concerning these we read, "Come now, you rich, weep and howl for the miseries that are coming upon you . . . Behold, the wages of the laborers who mowed your fields, which you kept back by fraud, cry out; and the cries of the harvesters have reached the ears of the Lord of hosts. You have lived on the earth in luxury and in pleasure; you have fattened your hearts in a day of slaughter" (James 5:1; 4–5). Perhaps there are not many Catholics reading this book who fall into this category, but it's always good to examine your conscience to see if you are somehow taking for yourself more than is just.

The second danger of wealth comes when those who have wealth are unwilling to help those who are in need. The parable of Lazarus and the rich man in the sixteenth chapter of Luke's Gospel speaks to this danger. Lazarus is not condemned for obtaining his wealth unjustly, but for failing to help one in need who was nearby. This sin of omission is so serious that the rich man finds himself in hell.

The third danger of wealth is the most insidious, and the one most likely to afflict even devout Catholics. It is the danger of making wealth a substitute for the providence of your Father in heaven. This is addressed in the twelfth chapter of Luke's Gospel in a parable Jesus tells about a man whose land produces an abundant harvest too great for his barns. At the end he is condemned for his behavior and his attitude toward God.

At first, we might be tempted to say that the problem with hoarding wealth or property is that it is the cause or result of injustices toward another. Perhaps the rich man is to be blamed because he acquired his wealth by stealing or by taking advantage of workers. But there is no evidence whatsoever of such a charge being brought against the man in the parable. The land is his; the produce is his; there is no mention of underpaid labor. Perhaps there was someone in need nearby who is neglected by the rich man, as happened with Lazarus and the rich man. But here again, there is no mention of this man neglecting someone in need. He seems to be blameless on both charges of injustice or neglect.

Yet God does blame him. And why? Because he "lays up treasure for himself and is not rich toward God." The problem with this man is that he has substituted his wealth for trust in God's providence. And so he is no longer in communion with his Father. Imagine a family in which one of the children hoards the food that the father daily provides and stores it in his room. Then one day the child stops coming to meals altogether and just stays in his room eating the food he has stored up. This would be an indication of a serious lack of trust in the heart of the child, and a failure to appreciate that this relationship of trust with his father is more important than the food itself. He fears that one day the food will stop appearing on the table, so he makes plans for the doomsday future he has imagined. Put simply, he does not trust that his father will continue to provide for him.

And this is perhaps the greatest danger that wealth poses to our souls: not injustice, not neglect of the poor, but substituting our wealth for the providence of our Father in heaven. We say to God with our lips, "I trust in you," but then we make a safety net out of our possessions just in case our Father will not catch us when we fall.

See how different the life of the poor man is from the life of the rich man. The poor man every day comes to his Father with his hands empty, asking this day for his daily bread. I cannot help thinking of the beautiful character Tevye from *Fiddler on the Roof*. He is a man in constant communion with God, for he has no other choice. How pleased the Father is that his children come to him trustingly each day, knowing that were it not for him they could not provide for themselves. The rich man may pray, "Give us this day our daily bread," yet he knows full well where today's bread is, and tomorrow's bread, and the next day's. For such a one there is no risk, no real need to trust, and hence no deep communion with the Father.

I once read a remarkable story told by a woman named Gloria Polo. She had been struck by lightning, and while she hovered between life and death she had a vision of a man whose prayers saved her soul from damnation. In her account she writes about a poor country farmer in South America who had his small farm raided by soldiers who stole his chickens and burned his crops. He had nothing left for his family but two paper bills: one of 5,000 pesos, the other 10,000. But he went to Church still, giving thanks to God in the midst of his misfortune. He put into the collection basket the 10,000-peso bill, and with the other bill he bought a loaf of bread for his family, trusting that God would take care of him. The bread was wrapped in newspaper, and in the newspaper he read about a woman who had been struck by lightning and was in danger of death. So he prayed for her, and because he was so full of childlike trust, his prayers for the salvation of souls was very powerful in God's sight and the woman's life was saved.

To be like this man is to be like a little child who completely depends upon his parents for his every need. So we can see how covetousness, the attachment to wealth, harms our union with the Father and impedes purity of heart.

My own father was an extraordinary example of generosity to me and my brother. I never saw him pass a poor person without stopping to give him something. If we were driving in a car and on the opposite side of the road my father saw a homeless man, he would make a U-turn in order to give him something. Once, when I was a teenager, we visited Tijuana. From the United States into Mexico there is a footbridge and on that bridge, beginning on the Mexican side, there were hundreds of beggars, each with a paper cup asking for money. I thought to myself, *Finally! Dad is going to pass a poor person and not give him anything.*

Boy, was I wrong.

My father saw all those poor people, turned around and went to a bank on the U.S. side. He cashed a $100 bill into quarters, and stopped and gave every single beggar on that bridge something. At the time I was very irritated, but now I look back on my irritation with contrition. I now realize that during all the years when Jesus sat begging in the persons of those hundreds of beggars, he never met anyone as generous as my father. I think it is safe to say that my father spent most of our inheritance on the poor. But he gave to my brother and me a much greater inheritance: an example of extraordinary generosity. And for that I am eternally grateful.

Someone might read this and ask if the teaching of the Lord to avoid covetousness prohibits saving money and making future plans. No; this is right and prudent. But the teaching does forbid us to be anxious about our plans as if we could wholly control our own fate. St. Thomas teaches:

> Although it is in our power to act, yet it is not in our power that our actions attain to their due ends on account of the impediments that can happen. And so, that which each one attains by his action lies subject to the disposition of the divine [will]. Therefore, the Lord commands us not to be solicitous about those things the care of which pertain to God, namely, the outcomes of our actions. God does not, however, prohibit us to be solicitous about those things that pertain to us, namely about our work...Hence, he does not prohibit that we store up those things that are necessary for us tomorrow in their time, but [he prohibits] that we be solicitous about future events with a certain desperation of the divine help, or lest we be preoccupied today with the solicitude which we will have to have tomorrow.[16]

Carrying the Cross

Ultimately, seeking first the kingdom of God means placing our whole hope for happiness in the Lord. And this means that

---

16 *Summa Contra Gentiles*, Bk. III, c.135.

we should not be surprised when the goods of this life fail us. Jesus taught us that at the end of every human life there waits a Calvary, and on the way to that Calvary we must pick up our cross and follow him. Your children must come to understand this about their faith. Otherwise they will grow disillusioned and think that their faith has failed to provide them with the goods it promised. Sometimes, very heavy crosses come very early in a child's life: the tragic death of a parent or loved one, a debilitating illness, or the like. These moments of crisis are also moments of decision: the decision to place all our hopes in the life to come, or the decision to despair of ever being happy.

Does this decision to place all of our hope for happiness in the next life mean that we will just have to be miserable in this life? Not at all. On the contrary: the one who places his hope for happiness in the life to come will be happier in *this* life than if he sought happiness only in this life. For hope in the goods of the future life causes joy to be present now, much as the person who wins the lottery is filled with joy even while he holds the ticket before he has received the payment.

A simple parable will serve to illustrate what I mean. Imagine that you have a dear friend, someone whom you love as your own self. When you are together, you are always happy, and when you are apart you are sad. And it happens that the Lord gives you a choice. On the one hand, you can be constantly together with your friend for some weeks or months or even years, but after that time you will forever be separated from your friend. Or, on the other hand, you can be apart from your friend for some weeks or months, or even years, but after that time you will always and forever be together with your friend. Which of the two would you choose? It is obvious that you would choose the second. Why? Because if you chose the first, even the time you were together with your friend would be seasoned with bitterness because of the impending and inevitable separation. So you couldn't even enjoy the time you were together. But if you chose the second, even the time you were apart from your friend would be seasoned with joy because of your anticipation of the inevitable, permanent reunion.

In fact, our present joy on account of our hope for future goods will be greater than the joy we would have had in the actual possession of temporal goods. The hopeful Christian is more joyful in this life than the man who possesses all the goods of this world. Not only that, but the longer we live the greater our joy becomes. We should be marking off the days of the calendar with our joy increasing after every passing day that we come closer to eternity.

I remember once as a teenager coming across a poem that an elderly nun used to recite as she did her knitting. It went like this:

> One day more of work for Jesus
> One day less of life for me
> But heaven is nearer
> And Christ is dearer
> Than yesterday to me.

That very beautifully expresses the sentiments of the Christian heart. If we choose to put our hopes and find our joy in the passing things of this world, then we will inevitably find disappointment. We will be like those who chose the first option: to be with the one we love only for a short time only to be separated from him forever. But if we place all our hope in the life to come, in Christ, then we are like those who chose the second option: to be separated from the one we love for a short time, only to be reunited with him forever.

So as a parent, how do you model that "kingdom-first" attitude? You do so *interiorly* by a disposition of trust during uncertain times, so that instead of expressing anxieties and fear, you speak calmly about accepting God's will and providence for your family. You model it *exteriorly* by generosity that reflects a deep compassion for the poor and a love for the work of the Church.

CHAPTER 5

Stress Doing Good More Than Avoiding Evil

The title of this chapter may seem nonsensical. After all, isn't doing good avoiding evil and isn't avoiding evil doing good? Aren't they two sides of the same coin?

Well, not exactly. Doing good is not just avoiding evil; it is not something merely negative. It involves a positive love and striving *for* something. The primary focus of our spiritual life needs to be on the good. Our avoidance of evil is really a consequence of our striving for good. But as a parent, it is often easier to see and correct your children's faults than it is to notice and encourage where they are taking initiative to act well. So, as I will try to manifest in this chapter, it is important to put your focus in training your children on the *primacy of doing good*.

It is true that early on in the spiritual life, it is natural for us to focus on avoiding evil. But even in this early stage of the spiritual life, we must not lose sight of the primacy of the good. The first of all the commandments does not begin with the words "thou shalt not," but rather "thou shalt love." And the Lord Jesus, when he promulgates the New Law in his Sermon

on the Mount, places the heart of the New Law in the Beatitudes; that is, in happiness. The human heart cannot be satisfied
by fear of evil. It was created by God for happiness, and so
the first moving principle of the human heart must be love of
happiness.

It's possible for us to understand this, yet in a particular case
where there is both a good to be sought, and an evil to be
avoided, be at a loss to determine whether it is more important to seek the good or avoid the evil. Often the possibility of
achieving a good is uncertain, and there may even be a risk of
falling into evil while striving for that good.

In the Gospels, Jesus tells two similar parables that both teach
us that in such cases it is more important to do good than to
avoid evil. One parable is from Matthew 25, the other is from
Luke 19. The parable from St. Matthew's Gospel reads:

> [The kingdom of heaven] will be as when a man go-
> ing on a journey called his servants and entrusted to
> them his property; to one he gave five talents, to an-
> other two, to another one, to each according to his
> ability. Then he went away. He who had received the
> five talents went at once and traded with them; and
> he made five talents more. So also, he who had the
> two talents made two talents more. But he who had
> received the one talent went and dug in the ground
> and hid his master's money. Now after a long time the
> master of those servants came and settled accounts
> with them. And he who had received the five tal-
> ents came forward, bringing five talents more, saying,
> "Master, you delivered to me five talents; here I have
> made five talents more." His master said to him, "Well
> done, good and faithful servant; you have been faithful
> over a little, I will set you over much; enter into the joy
> of your master." And he also who had the two talents
> came forward, saying, "Master, you delivered to me
> two talents; here I have made two talents more." His

master said to him, "Well done, good and faithful servant; you have been faithful over a little, I will set you
over much; enter into the joy of your master." He also
who had received the one talent came forward, saying,
"Master, I knew you to be a hard man, reaping where
you did not sow, and gathering where you did not
winnow; so I was afraid, and I went and hid your talent
in the ground. Here you have what is yours."

But his master answered him, "You wicked and sloth-
ful servant! You knew that I reap where I have not
sowed, and gather where I have not winnowed? Then
you ought to have invested my money with the bank-
ers, and at my coming I should have received what was
my own with interest. So take the talent from him, and
give it to him who has the ten talents. For to every one
who has will more be given, and he will have abundance; but from him who has not, even what he has
will be taken away. And cast the worthless servant into
the outer darkness; there men will weep and gnash
their teeth" (25:14-30).

What is the sin of the lazy servant? He is faced with a choice:
either he can put effort into trying to do a good, with the risk
that he might fail (trading his talent); or he can simply avoid an
evil without effort or risk of failure (burying his talent). In the
end, he is more afraid of doing evil than of omitting good. This
reveals that the spiritual life is primarily about doing good, not
primarily about avoiding evil.[17] So one lesson we can learn

---

17 It seems to me that the inability to see this truth is one of the marks of scrupu-
    losity. The scrupulous person is obsessed with avoiding evil, even if this means
    omitting great good. For example, he will omit receiving Communion out of
    fear of sacrilege, even if there is little evidence that he has sinned gravely. For
    the scrupulous person, God is a harsh master to be defended against by means
    of a contract, not a generous father who is to be approached with confidence
    and gratitude. For the scrupulous person, salvation is not joy, but merely relief.

from this parable is that it is important to take risks for the sake of doing good.

Let us look at some concrete examples. A young man struggles with impure thoughts, and although he has tried to push them out of his mind, he is not certain whether or not he has given consent to these thoughts. So when he goes to Mass, he has a choice to make: he fears committing the sin of sacrilege but also he desires the good of being united to Christ in Holy Communion. Since it is more important to do good than to avoid evil, he should make an act of contrition and take the risk of approaching Jesus in Holy Communion.[18] In another case, a young person is thinking about his vocation. He may desire marriage or some form of consecrated life, but he is afraid to try either for risk of failing, since the demands of marriage and consecrated life seem very difficult. Once again, in such a case, he ought to take the risk of doing good, pursuing the vocation to which he thinks he is called, even in the face of the possibility of failure.

But that brings us to another question: what about the risk? Why isn't there a story about a servant who trades and loses his master's money? Here again, what the parable doesn't say is as instructive as what it does say. I think that the fact that there is no servant who trades and fails is an indication of the *generosity of God*, who does not permit those who try to serve him to fail in doing spiritual good.

It may be that they seem to lack success from the point of an external observer; but God calls us to be faithful, not successful in the eyes of the world. So long as we seek to do God's will with love, we cannot fail to grow in love. Unlike physical goods, spiritual goods multiply simply by being exercised. And

---

18 Of course, this is for the case where someone is uncertain if he has fallen into serious sin. If someone is morally certain that they have committed a serious sin, they should make a sacramental confession before approaching sacramental Communion.

therefore what seems like a risk from the viewpoint of the servant is destined always to succeed from the viewpoint of the master, who always gives more than enough to his servants: "For God is at work in you, both to will and to work for his good pleasure" (Phil. 2:13).

And so, lying beneath the truth that it is more important to do good than to avoid evil is a more fundamental truth: God is not a harsh judge who is looking out for our every misstep. On the contrary, he is a loving Father who is always on our side, always looking out for the least good action we do, and always assisting our desires and intentions to do good. St. Faustina describes a conversation between Jesus and a soul on the point of despair. In that conversation, she recounts how God assists this soul so long as it is willing to do even the least good:

> Jesus calls to the soul a third time, but the soul remains deaf and blind, hardened and despairing. Then the mercy of God begins to exert itself, and, without any co-operation from the soul, God grants it final grace. If this too is spurned, God will leave the soul in this self-chosen disposition for eternity. This grace emerges from the merciful heart of Jesus and gives the soul a special light by means of which the soul begins to understand God's effort; but conversion depends on its own will. The soul knows that this, for her, is final grace and, should it show even a flicker of good will, the mercy of God will accomplish the rest.[19]

God is our Father! He is rooting for us! After all the signs of his love for us, after he has even given life of his only-begotten Son in exchange for ours, how can we continue to disbelieve in his goodness and love for us? Jesus is always telling parables in which he laments that we have less confidence in God than

---

19 Diary, n. 1486.

in an unjust judge (Luke 18) or an evil human father (Luke 11). We think he cares for us less than the grass of the field or the birds of the air (Matt. 6).

Parents, do not give the impression to your children that God is a hard master. Instead, encourage in them the attitude of primarily seeking the good, not avoiding evil. When you teach your children, do not focus exclusively or even primarily on avoiding sin. Stress the importance of seeking and loving the good. When you punish your children, do not be as severe with those who fail in their attempts to do good as you are with those who refuse to attempt the good. Do not be for your children the image of a hard master, but rather of our loving God.

In one of the U.S. Marine handbooks, there is an instruction about encouraging initiative among soldiers:

> In practical terms, this means that we must not strive for certainty before we act, for in so doing we will surrender the initiative and pass up opportunities. We must not try to maintain excessive control over subordinates since this will necessarily slow our tempo and inhibit initiative.[20]

A corollary of this is that those who fail after taking initiative are not to be disciplined as severely as those who fail to take initiative. This is sound advice not only for captains but also for parents.

---

20 Fleet Marine Force Manual 1, *Warfighting*, p. 81.

CHAPTER 6

Protect Your Children from Evil Influences

---　※

This chapter is both unnecessary and necessary. It is unnecessary to inform Catholic parents that they need to protect their children from harmful influences because you already understand that well. But it is necessary because often parents are not aware of many of the hidden harms that exist in their children's world. As a priest I have seen, time and time again, even very young children harmed by things that their parents never suspected were dangers.

The need to keep a distance from worldly culture has been part of Christian teaching from the beginning. In his first homily on Pentecost Sunday, St. Peter warns the people, "Save yourselves from this crooked generation" (Acts 2:40). Some parents think this means circling the wagons and keeping their children from any contact with the world outside their family. But although this might be necessary in some extreme cases, it comes with collateral damage: stunted psychic and spiritual maturity. Human beings are naturally social animals, and so we can only find our full perfection in the context of a society larger than the family. (The fact that we must find a spouse outside of our family is evidence for this.) So the challenge for most Catholic parents is how to simultaneously protect your children from the harmful influences of a corrupt society while exposing them to the necessary goods that only a society can bring.

In this chapter I will attempt to identify the most significant sources of hidden harm to children, while at the same time give suggestions for helping your children embrace what is good and necessary for their development.

But before I do that, there is an important principle that you have to put in place when determining how to protect your children from harm. The principle is this: *the human heart cannot live in a vacuum*. If you take away something from children that they consider to be good, their heart will seek something else to fill the void. So if, for the sake of protecting your children from harmful influences, you restrict their activities or access to certain things, make sure you give them healthy and satisfying replacements so they can pursue legitimate goods. If you tell them to stay off the internet, then get them involved in something else they really enjoy, such as sports, reading, drawing, or writing. If you tell them to cut off bad friendships, make sure you give them the opportunity to form new, healthy friendships. With that in mind, here are some areas in which a parent ought to be very vigilant.

The Internet and Other Media

Although nearly everyone today recognizes the dangers of the internet, most parents who are over forty have not fully grasped the ways in which the internet can harm their children. For parents of this age group, the internet did not exist when they were children. It was something they first encountered as mature adults, and by then they already had sufficient awareness and moral habits that serve as a kind of built-in caution against the dangers of the internet. Parents from this generation are thus simply not suspicious enough to protect their children sufficiently.

My experience as a priest tells me that most young people get exposed to harmful things online, such as pornography, before they are even teenagers. And this exposure can lead to serious moral problems that greatly discourage young people and lead them to despair of being able to keep the moral teachings of the Church.

With regard to pornography, parents should realize that the internet is not passive. It is always fishing for children. A child may be looking at a perfectly legitimate site, but in a sidebar or in the ads there is something funny or interesting designed to catch the attention of a child. A few clicks can lead to another set of sidebars or ads that are salacious or immodest. From there, explicitly pornographic (and often violent) photos and videos may be just a short surf away—sometimes even disguised as something else to attract a child's curiosity.

Pornography is not the only danger with which the internet threatens children. There are also other serious dangers. For example, there are child abusers posing as other children, offering friendship and companionship; false teachers who try to fill the minds of young people with harmful doctrines; financial scams; and, of course, all manner of profane entertainments that harm the spirit.

These days, most parents recognize the need to have passwords and other protections on their computers, but because they are often not as up to date on technology as their children, they do not realize the many loopholes that can circumvent those protections. For example, not long ago I was speaking to a friend of mine who has teenage sons. I asked him if he had everything carefully monitored, and he assured me that he had. For example, his sons only had flip phones that did not have internet access. I then asked him, "Do the phones allow photo attachments with text messages?" He said they probably did, but he didn't suspect that would be a problem until I persuaded him that it could be. A couple of weeks after he made sure the phones could not receive images, a member of his son's soccer team sent out a group text message with a violent pornographic image attached, and his son was the only one on the team who didn't see it.

The moral of such stories is that you need to be suspicious in a healthy way, ceaselessly vigilant. You should also avail yourself of the knowledge of experts to make sure your measures to protect your kids keep up with the threats and the technological developments. It is a serious inconvenience sometimes, but your children's innocence and safety are worth it.

Bad Friendships and Romantic Relationships

Another way that children are tempted to abandon the practice of their Catholic faith is through bad friendships, especially bad romantic relationships. St. Paul warns frankly, "Do not be deceived: 'Bad company ruins good morals'" (1 Cor. 15:33). Friendship is one of the greatest goods of human life, and one of the most important steps in a young person's life is the formation of his own friendships. But it is important that these friendships are not parallel relationships that exist in isolation from your family relationships. The most healthy friendships and relationships are integrated into the existing family relationships that young people already have. When they are otherwise, two very important elements of a person's life can come into conflict and cause one or the other (for teenagers, usually the family) to be rejected.

The best situation is where Catholic families form family friendships with other, like-minded Catholic families. This provides a healthy social setting for socializing children in a context larger than the immediate family and also creates opportunities for strong, loving relationships to form, reinforcing the virtues and the faith of children.

A particular difficulty arises with regard to romantic relationships. The age at which reproduction is possible is typically in the early teens, sometimes as early as twelve or thirteen years old. This is an indication that nature intends members of our species to reproduce shortly after this age. Nevertheless, our culture is such that the requirements of providing for a family and of acquiring the requisite knowledge and virtues for family life often are not possible until the early twenties. And so there is about a ten-year gap between the natural inclination to marry and the circumstances in which marriage is reasonable.

All this means that much self-discipline will be required on the part of young persons dating members of the opposite sex, and much prudence and discernment on the part of parents. As one experienced father of a large family counseled me, "Raising a teenager is like catching a fifty-pound fish with a five-pound line."

One of the most important things you can do is to make sure your children invite their friends, especially persons of romantic interest, over to your home. This at once assures your children that you are open to permitting them to form friendships with people outside your family and also allows you to evaluate the quality of their relationships. (It also helps build integration, rather than division, between their friendships and their family life.) If you can tell that the friendships are healthy and that their families are healthy, then you can consider allowing your children to visit the homes of their friends.

Advice for Courtship

Courtship, or dating, is a necessary and beautiful stage in the development of the person who is seeking to fulfil a vocation to marriage. A child who witnesses the love of his father and mother beholds that spousal communion from the outside. Of course, by the time your children begin to seriously discern marriage, they will be young adults and will likely be living outside of the home. So the advice I am providing here is primarily useful in speaking to your adolescent children about dating in the future. However, it can also be helpful when your adult children seek counsel from you after they have left the home.

Through courtship, a person begins to *enter into* a communion like that found between spouses. This entering into communion with a member of the opposite sex is both a time of discernment and of personal growth in the capacity for self-giving in the manner proper to spouses. Therefore, the first principle of courtship is that it is ordained toward discerning marriage. Dating is not a form of entertainment or self-gratification, nor is it a means of balancing loneliness with the desire for freedom and self-determination.[21] Just to be clear: I am speaking here about dating as *courtship*—an overtly exclusive and romantic relationship. There are, of course, more preliminary relationships that are not exclusive, such as spending time with friends of the opposite sex in groups or even one-on-one dates in which a man and woman are trying to get to know each other better.

Because dating is ordered to discerning marriage, dating should not begin in earnest until the possibility of marriage is on the horizon. In my experience, a good rule of thumb is that exclusive, one-on-one dating should begin about two years from the time when someone could reasonably expect

---

21 Often, a person starts a relationship, or remains in one, because he wants occasional companionship—not because he is looking toward a lifelong communion. Many people don't want be lonely but also don't want to lose their freedoms by entering into a serious commitment. But of course, a right understanding of courtship and marriage sees that freedom is not sacrificed, but rather enhanced by entering into a more profound communion with others. The young man who gives up his ability to go out whenever he pleases when he gets married also gains the ability to beget and raise children by that same act. So he exchanges a lesser freedom for a greater freedom. Freedom is the ability to act in a way that perfects one's nature, and raising a family perfects human nature more than being able to go where one pleases when one pleases.

to marry. If the time of courtship goes much longer than two years, the likelihood of exceeding the boundaries of reasonable affection grows significantly.

Although dating is a beginning of entering into spousal communion, it is important that the couple clearly understand the boundaries between the communion proper to dating and the communion proper to marriage. Obviously, sexual intercourse is proper only to the married state, since it is ordered to the generation of children. Cohabitation and sexual intimacy before marriage, aside from being serious sins, can have lasting negative effects into the marriage itself. First of all, the couple have already engaged in the acts proper to marriage so that often they are confused about what makes them truly married. They think that marriage means a promise to live with one another for the rest of their lives, or to love one another for the rest of their lives, or to raise children together. But none of these makes someone married. After all, unmarried persons might do all of these and they still would not be married.

In marriage, by a solemn and lifelong vow the spouses give to one another the exclusive right over each other's bodies for acts apt to generate children. If the couple has already been sexually intimate before the marriage, they can become habitually blinded to the truth that marriage and exclusive sexual intimacy go hand-in-hand. The husband may have greater difficulty in trusting that his wife is faithful to him, and the wife may tend to suspect her husband of seeking self-gratification even when he asks for legitimate sexual intimacy after marriage. For couples who were sexually intimate before marriage, the overall effect is that the blessings of marital intercourse are diminished. It is as if they had mortgaged their marital intimacy before the marriage ever took place, and their experience of sexual intimacy in the marriage is impoverished.

Not only sexual intercourse, but also close physical intimacy (intimate touching, passionate kissing, etc.) which, in itself, *inclines* the emotions toward sexual intercourse, is also proper to married communion only. Another form of excessive familiarity to help your children avoid is spending a long time together alone in a private residence, or spending time alone together late at night or early in the morning in a private place. Even if such excessive familiarity were not an occasion of sin, this kind of living on familiar terms is one of the blessings of married life. To share a life so as to live together in the same home is proper to the communion of family life. And when a dating couple appropriates this kind of familiarity to themselves before marriage, they no longer experience it as a blessing proper to marriage. Instead, it is "just what couples do." On the other hand, couples who reserve this kind of living on familiar terms to their marriage experience this form of intimacy as one of the blessings of marriage. In this way, the marriage bond is strengthened for both.

Some exaggerated forms of piety require that a dating couple show no more interest or affection toward each other than a brother and a sister. But this is clearly contrary to the aim of dating. A brother and sister could never discern marriage, so their interaction must have an essentially different character than a couple who is discerning marriage. For example, an intimate conversation about how to raise children together would not be appropriate for a brother and sister, but would be a necessary conversation for couples discerning marriage. Outward signs of affection and some form of exclusivity in the relationship are appropriate, so long as they are not in themselves ordered to (or likely to produce) sexual desire.[22]

---

22 Sometimes an innocent gesture of affection, such as holding hands or a brief hug, arouses sexual desire. Such things are not in themselves disordered signs of affection, but if sexual desire comes about, the person in whom the desire comes about should discretely discontinue the affection until the desire goes away. It's not necessary thereafter always to avoid such licit signs of affection in the future, since such things often depend upon bodily dispositions that frequently change. Licit signs of affection are good and important signs of love, so we should not be scrupulous and teach children to omit such licit and wholesome signs of love out of fear that some evil not intrinsically connected to the affection might come about.

Since dating is ordered toward marriage, the discernment involved in dating should focus upon the compatibility of a man and woman for coming together to form a family. This presupposes that each person possess the requisite knowledge and moral virtues to enter freely and permanently into a marriage and provide for children. It also means that the two persons complement one another in the goods that are proper to marriage and family life. For example, if two persons are significantly unequal, say in education, or culture, or maturity, this can be a serious impediment to marriage, in which spouses are supposed to relate to one another as equals, not like a parent to a child.

This discernment process will be greatly assisted if both parties are open and docile to the advice of their parents or others who know and love them well. Strong emotions tend to predominate between a young man and woman, and without such guidance this can greatly obscure their ability to accurately judge their compatibility for marriage.

In a healthy courtship, the love of the man and woman for each other is not in competition with their love for God, but serves in a certain sense as a springboard for a greater appreciation of God's goodness found in the other. The goodness of the other is seen as having its origin in God, so that each person spontaneously moves from a love and appreciation of their beloved to a greater love and appreciation for God's goodness found in their beloved.

Perhaps the best sign that a relationship is suited for marriage is that the concrete practice of love for God in each person is enhanced by the relationship, not diminished by it. And conversely, if dating or engagement results in a diminishment of the concrete practice of charity toward God, then this is a sign that the couple is not suited for marriage. For example, if a young man or woman is in the habit of attending daily Mass, but after they begin dating they no longer have time for Mass, this is a sign that they are not leading one another closer to

Christ. Jesus warns against this in Luke 14:20, when he mentions a man who refuses to go to the great banquet because he has just gotten married.

Sex Education and Indoctrination in Schools

Another area where parents are often unaware of threats to their children's Catholic faith is in education that takes place outside the home. As we noted earlier, since the industrial revolution, education has largely been delegated to non-family members outside the home. Parents often assume that the education their children are receiving is similar to or at least analogous with the education they received. But, in fact, this is largely untrue. The radical shift in the culture has resulted in a radical shift in educational philosophy, and part of that new educational philosophy involves the denial that the parents are the primary educators of their children. One consequence of this is that many states have laws that permit schools to refrain from disclosing to parents the content of classroom teaching or even from letting parents know about certain behaviors of their children. In many places, public educators are empowered to encourage and conceal homosexual behavior, cross-dressing, the use of contraceptives, and even abortions.

It is probably safe to say now that the public educational system—from grade school through graduate school—has become an accessory to indoctrination of anti-Christian principles. And it is not just the official teaching authorities in these schools who promote anti-Christian views, it is also the other students with whom your children will associate and make friendships.

We live now in a time and place where the words of the Lord ring true: "If the world hates you, know that it has hated me before it hated you. If you were of the world, the world would love its own; but because you are not of the world, but I chose you out of the world, therefore the world hates you. Remember the word that I said to you, 'A servant is not greater than his master.' If they persecuted me, they will persecute you; if they kept my word, they will keep yours also" (John 15:18-20).

How should Catholic parents respond to this situation? The first step is for you to recognize the gravity of the situation. The world your children are growing up in is not the world you grew up in—even if your childhood feels like it was not very long ago—nor are the morals of today's society the same. If you send your children to public school, you must constantly take the initiative to find out what your children are learning and hearing. If they have been taught anti-Catholic positions, you must take the time to discuss these views patiently and intelligently with your children, contrasting them with the truths of the Faith, helping them to resist error while witnessing to the truth. You must be extra-vigilant in guarding your children against secretive and unhealthy friendships.

When it comes to sex education, which public schools are imposing on children at ever-younger ages and in ever-more-salacious detail, you must take bold steps to protect your kids' innocence. *Children should not be exposed to sex education at any school, at any level.* That education is a sacred duty and right of parents. Fathers should be especially proactive in speaking to their sons, and mothers likewise with their daughters, about the specifics of sexual love. Sons ought to learn how to be a man from their father, and girls ought to learn how to be a woman from their mother.

And still, a certain reverence and modesty should be observed about the details of procreation even between parents and their children. Nature has equipped our species (as every species) with the instinctual knowledge of the details of procreation once the proper setting is in place. The instruction of the parents should focus primarily upon indicating what the proper setting is for marital intimacy, and the moral disposition with which to approach matters of sexual chastity. The parents should not primarily focus on the details of the biological mechanics of reproduction.

Finally, parents must understand that the education of your children is precisely the common activity that constitutes the reason for your marriage. The more intentional you are about directly cooperating in the education of your children, the stronger your marriage will become. No one cares about your children as much as you do. And that means the care of your children belongs to *you*. A first option that parents should investigate is to educate their children at home. This may be difficult, but it is fitting, since you are the primary educators of your children. Fortunately, there are many homeschooling programs that have excellent curricula as well as teaching assistance.[23]

At some point, however, every parent needs to enlist help for more advanced academic education. In such cases, the first thing to look for is a good Catholic school nearby. Preferably, Catholic education should extend through college. Catholic education does not end when your child turns eighteen. I have met many parents who thought that their children were sufficiently well-formed by the end of high school, and then sent their children to a secular college, only to find out that their children were incapable of dealing with the intellectual and moral attacks on their faith. A typical college professor can raise problems that even a well-catechized high school student is incapable of resolving. And though there are exceptions, it is much safer to send your children to an authentically Catholic college than to a secular institution of higher learning. We will look more closely at Catholic higher education in the next chapter.

---

23 For a list of Catholic homeschool programs, see: https://a2zhomeschooling. com/religion/catholic_home_school/catholic_homeschooling_programs/

CHAPTER 7

Don't Let "Catholic" Schools Steal Their Faith

✳

When my father was a chemistry major at Notre Dame in the mid-1950s, he was required (as were all Notre Dame students) to take the core religion courses. Catholic priests with advanced degrees taught him that the main thing someone had to do to be a faithful Catholic was to take care of the poor (a teaching he took completely to heart, much to his credit). They also taught him that there was no devil and no hell. (God loves everyone too much for that kind of thing.) According to those priests, fidelity to the teaching of the Church in faith or morals (especially sexual morals) was optional, and sometimes even harmful to living life as an authentic disciple of Christ.

Not surprisingly, my father stopped practicing his faith, and he stopped believing in some of the most fundamental doctrines handed down from Christ to the Church through his apostles. As a consequence, my brother and I were not raised Catholic. (Thanks be to God, we found our way into the Catholic Church by God's providential care—but that's another story).

My father's story is not unique or even rare, and it illustrates something that many Catholics have been in denial about for decades. The Catholic education system in the United States is broken. And the problem did not begin, as some assume, with the Second Vatican Council. Notre Dame was the flagship Catholic university in the United States, and yet the most pernicious heresies were being disseminated in the core religion courses there even, in the 1950s, under the pseudo-authority of priests with the highest academic credentials. How was that possible?

I do not know how things are at Notre Dame today. Better, I hope—and I don't mean to single it out for blame. But Notre Dame is a symbol of what happened to nearly all of Catholic education in the United States beginning in the first half of the twentieth century.

The challenges that parents face in providing their children with an authentic Catholic education can extend all the way from grammar school to university. The most serious problems seem to have begun at the university level and then trickled down to secondary and finally to primary education, so each of these levels merits some consideration.

Difficulties with University Level Catholic Education

In 1967, the heads of several prominent Catholic colleges (including Notre Dame, Georgetown, and Fordham) came together in Land O'Lakes, Minnesota to hold a conference on the future course of Catholic education. The result of that conference was the "Land O'Lakes Statement," which rejected Church teaching on the nature and purpose of Catholic education in the name of "institutional autonomy and academic freedom." Among other things, the statement implicitly rejected the truth of revelation as handed down from Christ and the apostles as well as the teaching authority of the Church in matters of faith and morals. The ripple effects of this document devastated the Catholic higher educational landscape, and some of the universities that were represented at the Land O'Lakes Conference have since renounced their Catholic faith altogether.

From its opening paragraph, the statement reveals a studied ambiguity, viewing every kind of authority as a violent intrusion upon the legitimate freedom that arts and sciences ought to enjoy. But such a view of authority implicitly presupposes that every authority is fallible and, moreover, has no overarching wisdom to offer—wisdom that could illumine and assist the arts and sciences. In fact, there is a profound unity and order in the universe, and divine revelation harmonizes with right reason. Truth does not contradict truth, and authentic Catholic education presupposes that the revelation of Jesus Christ is true—thus "institutional autonomy and academic freedom" have nothing to fear from it.

The rejection of this principle resulted in many Catholic universities becoming incoherent. In one class they taught things consistent with the Catholic faith, while in the next class the contrary would be taught. Another effect was the disintegration of the curriculum. Authentic Catholic education considers sacred theology as the highest wisdom; the other arts and sciences ultimately contribute toward and lead up to it as a culmination of education, giving unity and order to the entire curriculum. But the principles laid out in the Land O'Lakes Statement disconnected other academic disciplines from the highest truths that made them coherent. The Catholic university became a secular cake with Catholic icing.

The crisis in Catholic education became so acute that, in 1990, John Paul II issued the apostolic constitution *Ex Corde Ecclesiae* mandating that teaching at Catholic colleges and universities be compatible with Catholic teaching.[24] Those who

---

24 "All Catholic teachers are to be faithful to, and all other teachers are to respect, Catholic doctrine and morals in their research and teaching. In particular, Catholic theologians, aware that they fulfil a mandate received from the Church, are to be faithful to the Magisterium of the Church as the authentic interpreter of Sacred Scripture and Sacred Tradition" (*Ex Corde Ecclesiae*, art. 4, section 3).

teach on matters of faith and morals were required to take an oath promising fidelity to the teachings of the Catholic Church. (At this time, thirty years later, only a handful of colleges and universities that bear the name "Catholic" have complied with the requirements of *Ex Corde Ecclesiae*.)

Difficulties in Secondary and Primary Education

The rejection of authentic Catholic educational principles at the university level has had a trickle-down effect into Catholic secondary and primary education. After all, not only were many of the high school and grade school teachers formed at Catholic universities, the books and curriculum for Catholic primary and secondary schools were being authored by graduates from them. So, you must also be proactive in inquiring about the books and teaching materials being used in your children's primary and secondary Catholic schools.

Another side effect of the rejection of Catholic faith and morals in education was the tolerance of teachers who lived lives in public opposition to Catholic faith and morals. In grade school and high school, the moral example of teachers plays no small part in a child's education. If a teacher is forthcoming about the aspects of his moral life that are contrary to Catholic teaching, this sows confusion and doubt in a child's mind about whether Catholic morality is important or just optional. After all, his parents have entrusted him to teachers at a Catholic school who openly reject Catholic morality.

My own family is a microcosm of the effects of Catholic education's decline and loss of fidelity. My cousins on my father's side of the family were all sent to Catholic schools for grade school, usually high school, and even college. Almost all of them ended up leaving the practice of their Catholic faith to some degree or another (although a few have slowly started coming back, thanks be to God). My brother and I were among the few who did not receive a Catholic education in our youth, and yet we were the only seriously practicing Catholics left. "Catholic" education not only did not help my family—it was positively harmful.

As a priest, I have heard this lament countless times from Catholic parents. "I sent my kids to Catholic school for twelve or sixteen years. I sacrificed and worked hard to pay for tuition. Why aren't they Catholic today?" More often than not, the short answer is: *because you are a victim of false advertising.* You sent them to schools that said they were Catholic but were not.

Fake vs Authentic Catholic Education

Given that many colleges and universities claim to be Catholic but are not, how can a parent discern which are truly Catholic and which are not? First of all, research the school's curriculum and read its literature and publications. If you find anything that is inconsistent with Catholic teaching, that is a red flag. Second, be willing to ask questions. Here are some questions to which every parent should know the answers before sending children to a Catholic college or university.

+ Are the people in charge serious, practicing Catholics?

+ Is there a requirement that all persons in leadership positions, whether they are Catholic or non-Catholic, abide by Catholic moral principles? For example, are those who are unmarried required to remain chaste outside of marriage, etc.

+ Is there a requirement that all persons in leadership positions, Catholic or non-Catholic, not publicly advocate for positions contrary to the teaching of the Catholic Church? For example, are they required to not publicly advocate for abortion or homosexual rights, etc.

+ Does the school make a point of having a Catholic *identity*, not just of coming from a "Catholic tradition"? A Catholic identity means that the school: 1) overtly professes fidelity to the teaching Church; 2) has a curriculum and policies that are consistent with Catholic doctrine; and 3) has a faculty largely composed of practicing Catholics. A Catholic tradition (in the pejorative sense used here) means that the school advertises itself as Catholic without having a true Catholic identity as I have described.

+ Does the school include courses that are apologetic in nature; that is, courses that raise contemporary objections to the Faith and help students answer them in a convincing manner?

+ What are the clubs permitted on campus? Are they consistent with a Catholic identity?

+ Are the majority of students practicing Catholics?

+ Do their teachers in faith and morals take an oath to abide by Catholic teaching (the *Mandatum* required by *Ex Corde Ecclesiae*)?

+ Does the college or university abide by the principle that accepting the teachings of the Catholic Church is not an impediment to authentic research and education?

+ Does the institution as a whole abide by Catholic moral teachings? For example, does its insurance cover abortion or contraception? Does it pay a just wage to its employees?

Before sending your children to a Catholic primary and secondary school, personally get to know those in the administration as well as those teachers who will directly educate your children. Ask yourself:

+ Are my children's teachers practicing Catholics? If not, do they teach their students anything contrary to the Catholic faith? Do they live in a way compatible with Catholic moral teaching?

+ Will my children be receiving "sex education" or any instruction about marriage and family issues without my prior knowledge and approval?

+ Will my children have an opportunity to attend Mass and go to confession regularly?

It may not be feasible, in your location and life circumstances, to send your child to a Catholic school with *all* the marks of an authentic Catholic educational institution. Nevertheless, you should know ahead of time just what sort of environment you are sending your children into, and be prepared to deal with potential problems that might arise as a result of its defects. Be upfront and informed! As in medicine, so in education: an ounce of prevention is worth a pound of cure. If you take the trouble to follow these steps, you will be able to discern a true Catholic school from a false one; true gold from fool's gold.

CHAPTER 8

Stay Calm If They Start to Question

———————————————————————————— ✳ ————————

There will come a time when your children begin to question certain elements of the Catholic faith, even elements that are fundamental. Don't panic—this is healthy and a necessary step in their own faith formation. John Henry Cardinal Newman once said, "Ten thousand difficulties do not make one doubt"[25] And the greatest theologian of the Catholic Church, St. Thomas Aquinas, relentlessly put the Faith to the test. Most of his works, in fact, are written in the form of questions—even about whether God exists or whether Jesus was God.

Faith is a gift from God, not something genetically inherited. This means that you must trust God to give faith to your children and ask him for this gift for each of your children even before they ever begin to question. Moreover, your children's faith is not just a borrowed version of your faith: they need to make it their own. Each person must come to a moment when he has to make his own act of faith. Your

————————————

25 *Apologia pro Vita Sua*, ch. 5.

children also have a responsibility to their conscience to reconcile what they know, or think they know, with the truths
definitively taught by Christ through his Church. And although this process is something deeply personal and in some
sense private, you can be a great assistance to your children in
getting through it.

This trust in God's work in the souls of your children is a
key component to keeping your kids Catholic. Raising children is not only about your children. It is about you. And by
that I don't only mean that it involves growing in the virtues
which make you a good parent. It also means growing in the
virtues which make you a better child of God. One of the key
elements in that relationship with God is to trust that he loves
your children more than you do, and that they are more truly
his than yours. Your relationship with your children gives you
a privileged perspective about how God sees and loves you *and*
your children.

When your children start questioning teachings of the
Church, the first thing to remember is: *stay calm.* Don't act
annoyed or angry. To the contrary, the best thing you can do
is respond patiently, in gentle tones, and even with a sense
of contentment that they are beginning to make their faith
their own. As a Catholic with a strong faith, you know that
everything revealed by God is true, so you should have no
fear that your children will somehow uncover some truth that
will overturn the teachings of the Church. You may not know
the answer to their questions, but someone does, and so you
can rest assured that the answers will be there if you look for
them diligently.

Next, sit down with them and explain the answers to their
difficulties as best you can. If there are questions for which you
do not know the answers (as inevitably there will be), send
them to a knowledgeable priest or to a good apologetics re-
source like Catholic Answers. In our day we're blessed with
an abundance of excellent books and websites for addressing

nearly every difficulty that someone might have concerning the teachings of the Catholic Church.

Discerning the Cause of Their Questions

It is also very important as a parent to figure out the underlying reason for their questions. Rarely are questions about the Faith purely academic and abstracted from the life experience, and this goes for your children, too. Some of their questions will really be motivated by concerns we've already addressed in earlier chapters. For example, the underlying cause of their difficulties may be family problems at home or differences in the faith of the parents, or negative associations with Catholicism due to a bad experience, or struggles with chastity that make the moral teachings of the Church seem burdensome. If these are the real issues, they should be addressed directly. Arguments will rarely have any effect since they will not address the underlying causes.

On the other hand, there will be times when the underlying cause for their difficulties will be something at the level of what they think is true or false. Here again, there are various ways in which this can happen. One common problem is that a young person thinks something is a part of the teaching of the Church when it is not. For example, someone might mistakenly think that the Church or the Bible teaches that the world was created in seven twenty-four-hour days and is only a few thousand years old.[26] Similar to such questions would be any questions about a seeming contradiction between science and

---

26 In this case, a brief survey of how the first Catholic theologians (called Fathers of the Church) dealt with these questions should be enough to overcome your children's difficulties. For example, St. Augustine points out that the sun was created on the fourth day, so the word "day" in that text of Genesis cannot possibly refer to one revolution of the sun around the earth. Augustine and St. Thomas Aquinas have very detailed explanations of the creation account in Genesis, which are perfectly consistent with what we know from science today.

revelation. Almost always, such apparent contradictions are the result of misunderstanding what revelation says or what science actually asserts with certitude. Cardinal Cesare Baronius put it succinctly when he said, "The Bible tells us how to go to heaven, not how the heavens go."[27]

Another source of misunderstanding is something called "intellectual custom"; that is, the habit of thinking in a certain way about things based upon what one is used to hearing. This habit makes people think that they know something to be true or false when in fact they do not know it: it is merely an opinion.

Sometimes it happens that intellectual custom is true. For example, I often ask my beginning students whether they know that the earth is round. Nearly all of them insist that this is something they know, and that it is not just something they believe. But upon questioning them about how they know it, their reason usually comes down to "everyone says it's true." I then show them how they could know it for a fact—for example, by circumnavigating the earth, or by witnessing a lunar eclipse where they can see that the earth casts a circular shadow on the face of the moon.

But often it happens that intellectual custom is false, and this is where many seeming conflicts arise with regard to the teachings of the Church. For example, a young person might think, as a matter of habit, that the purpose of marriage is the satisfaction of romantic feelings. This is a customary view in our times! Therefore, when such as person hears the Church teach that marriage is impossible between persons of the same sex, this seems manifestly to be both false and unjust, since persons of the same sex can feel romantic love toward each other.

The resolution involves explaining that the Church teaches that the purpose of marriage is not the satisfaction of romantic

---

27 This quote was attributed by Galileo to Cardinal Baronius in a letter he wrote to the Grand Duchess Christina in 1615. Some variation of it can be found, in substance, in Augustine's writings.

feelings but the generation and education of children.[28] So the Church has a completely different definition of marriage than what the prevailing intellectual custom presupposes. So to overcome this objection to Church teaching, and many others, involves more than presenting evidence and logic; it must begin by breaking down intellectual habits and presumptions that young people absorb from the culture around them, helping them to step outside their preconceived notions.

One way of helping them do this is to encourage the reading of books from different times and places. This will help your children distinguish between views that are really based in the evidence of their experience and views that are based merely upon what people around them say.

The Need to Trust in God

When all is said and done, making an act of faith involves trust in something you can't see. If God is really God, he must infinitely exceed the capacity of a created mind. So if we are to know some things about God and his intentions for creation, we will obviously have to take his word for it. But that raises the question: how do we know that it is his word?

The Catholic Church insists that there are objective

---

28 The fact that the Church permits infertile couples to enter into marriage is no obstacle to this. For even the marriage of infertile couples is for the purpose of the generation of children: that is why infertile couples must promise to one another the exclusive rights over one another's bodies for the acts apt to generate children. So long as they can do acts apt to generate children, they are entering into something for the sake of generating children. To be able to do something is not the same as to be for the sake of doing it. A blind eye is for the sake of seeing, even if it is unable to see. And a man who is unable to drive can get into a car, which is for the sake of driving. Similarly, someone who has an impeded natural ability to generate children can enter into a marriage which is for the sake of generating children. Besides the generation and education of children, there are also other goods aimed at in marriage, such as the mutual aid and communion of the spouses, and, in a Christian marriage, the signifying of the union of Christ and the Church. Marriage also provides a remedy for concupiscence, one of the principal effects of original sin.

evidences that allow someone to identify with some certitude that God has truly revealed himself in the person of Jesus Christ. God, in his goodness, does not require us to have blind faith without any objective evidence by which to gain probable knowledge of where to look for God's revelation. This evidence includes miracles, prophecies, and the witness of the lives of the saints, and you can use them all to help your children know that their Catholic faith is a faith that seeks understanding.

The abundance of miracles that testify to the truth of the Catholic faith is well-documented. Some are public miracles witnessed by so many people that no reasonable person could call them into question. For example, the miracle of the sun at Fátima was witnessed by 70,000, including non-believers who were converted by the experience. Other miracles specifically attest to particular truths of the Faith—for example, the many eucharistic miracles that have happened over the centuries until modern times. Beside these, there are the thousands of miracles of healing and the expulsion of demons for which there is ample testimony. Teach your children of any age about these miracles so that they can see that the supernatural character of the Catholic faith is not merely an assertion without basis.

Another kind of evidence for the truth and supernatural character of the Catholic faith is prophecy. Many prophecies and their fulfilments are found in the Bible; others are extrabiblical (for example, prophecies made by saints). Many biblical prophecies are so accurate and distinct that there is no reasonable explanation save that they were made by someone who knew the future, and that could only happen by divine power. For example, the prophecy of Psalm 22 about the exact manner of death of the Christ is so detailed that it must have a divine origin.[29] As for the many extrabiblical prophecies, these too are valuable but they must be examined with care. I recommend

---

29 The argument that the details of Jesus' death were made up to fit the prophecy is untenable since even the enemies of Jesus admitted that he died in this way. For example, the Jewish Talmud admits this.

only those prophecies given by canonized saints that have already been fulfilled.

Another kind of evidence for the truth and supernatural character of the Catholic faith that you can highlight for your questioning children is the *effect it has when fully lived*. The teachings of the Church ought to be judged by those who actually put them completely into practice—beginning with the saints, who are the ones who most fully believed and put them into practice. Other religions have notable characters, but not any of them hold a candle to the saints of the Church. If the teachings of the Church were false or fictitious, they would not likely produce saints, or so many saints. False ideas cause insanity, not sanctity. If your child sees that the worst that could happen from committing to the Catholic faith is to live a life exhibiting the joy, zeal, and good works of the saints, he is unlikely to see that faith as an impediment to his happiness!

Last of all, if for some reason your child finds the abundant testimony of so many miracles and prophecies unconvincing, try this argument from St. Thomas Aquinas:

> This wonderful conversion of the world to the Christian faith is so certain a sign of past miracles, that they need no further reiteration, since they appear evidently in their effects. It would be more wonderful than all other miracles, if without miraculous signs the world had been induced by simple and low-born men to believe truths so arduous, to do works so difficult, to hope for reward so high.[30]

That the whole world would have been converted by simpletons to a religion that makes the carrying of the cross and love of enemies mandatory requirements would be compelling enough on its own even if there were no miracles performed to convince people that this religion came from God.

---

30 *Summa Contra Gentiles*, I.6.

PART TWO

Helping Them Return to the Faith

CHAPTER 9

Respond Right
When Things Go Wrong

-- ✳ --------

If your children are happily practicing their faith today, you may think that the following chapters are not for you. But, the world being what it is, it is always good to be prepared. No matter how careful you are in raising your children, there will be influences outside of your control and even outside of your knowledge. What's more, your children have free will. So although it is not healthy to fret over what could go wrong, it is prudent to anticipate and prepare in the event that your children do go astray.

If you do have children who are not practicing their faith or are doing so lukewarmly and without zeal, then I hope that some of the things that follow will help you to help your children return to the joyful practice of their baptismal faith. There are, of course, different principles and strategies to employ depending upon whether your wayward children are adolescents or adults, and whether they live in your home or outside it. When applicable, I will try to make note of these differences.

One thing I often hear from parents is, "I don't know what

I did wrong! Why are my children away from God and the Faith?" If you have asked this question, the previous chapters may serve as a kind of examination of conscience for you. *Every* parent can find something (often many things) that he could have done better in raising his children, and that includes in raising them to be faithful Catholics. But remember what I said at the beginning of this book: even if you had done everything perfectly, your children have free will. Jesus was a perfect teacher and example of the Faith, yet he still lost one out of his twelve apostles.

So while you acknowledge your own shortcomings in raising your children, don't beat yourself up. It doesn't do any good for you or your children. You can't change the past, and beating yourself up about mistakes does not help your kids come back to the Church. God has permitted those mistakes in your past for a good reason, and he knows how to bring an even greater good out of them. So there is no sense in looking back on your life and wishing things had been different: "No one who sets a hand to the plow and looks to what was left behind is fit for the kingdom of God" (Luke 9:52).

Sometimes we confuse contrition with discouragement. Both are a kind of sorrow in response to our past sins. But contrition is a sorrow that gives us energy to get back up again and start over, whereas discouragement is a sorrow that makes us want to give up. Contrition is always from Christ, and discouragement is always from the devil. So if you feel discouragement, you must reject it like an evil spirit! Say it out loud if you have to: "I reject the spirit of discouragement!"

That being said, there is one simple thing you can do, looking ahead, to improve your relationship with your children. If you are aware of ways in which you have done wrong in raising your children (and who isn't?), don't be afraid to ask for their forgiveness. Meanwhile, let's look at some other common factors that lead to kids' falling away.

Depression

One of the most common evils from which modern young people suffer is depression. Depression can have many causes, some of which are avoidable and some of which are not. Over the years of my priesthood I have seen depression caused by traumatic childhood experiences such as moral disorders in the family, violence, or tragic accidents. I have seen depression caused by physiological or psychological causes such as bipolar disorder. I have seen depression caused by a person's own bad moral choices. I have even seen depression caused by direct demonic influence. It is essential to be able to identify the cause of the depression before seeking a solution. An experienced and holy priest together with a qualified mental health expert should be consulted in most cases.

The first response most people have to pain is to try to escape from it. But you should also listen to pain because it always tells you that something is wrong somewhere in your life. And it does no good to avoid the pain without heeding what it is telling you. One critical way to heed the suffering from depression, whether your own depression or the depression of someone you love, is to *pray*.

Scripture tells us that "being in agony, [Jesus] prayed more earnestly" (Luke 22:44). The apostles, on the other hand, slept in order to escape their sorrows, and so did not find the strength to do what was right (v. 45). It is hard to pray when you are sad, that is, when God most wants to give you the consolation that is a fruit of prayer. In Isaiah, God says, "For as the rain and the snow come down from heaven, and return not thither but water the earth, making it bring forth and sprout, giving seed to the sower and bread to the eater, so shall my word be that goes forth from my mouth; it shall not return to me empty, but it shall accomplish that which I purpose, and prosper in the thing for which I sent it" (55:10-11).

Here the "rain" signifies graces that come to the soul in
times of consolation, penetrating immediately into the soul
and bringing forth living things, namely the fruits of the Holy
Spirit. The "snow" signifies graces that come to the soul in
times of desolation. The soul, like the earth in winter, is hard,
and the snow does not penetrate or bring forth life immediately. But it remains upon the soul throughout the darkness and
cold until the rays of God's love begin to warm the soul, and
the snow is changed into life-giving water. In our spiritual life
we need to have not only rain but also snow. From where do
the rivers flow and the lakes receive replenishment during the
summer? From the melting snow on the mountains. So too,
during the summer heat, through the heat of temptations and
dryness, graces that were won during times of desolation and
coldness come to water and refresh the soul.

Sometimes young people identify the Church or the practice of their faith as the source of their depression. Almost always this happens because of a traumatic experience associated
with the Church. The most tragic of these are found in the
well-documented cases of clergy abuse. When someone has
been abused by a representative of the Church, it is quite natural for him to cease practicing the Faith, which he sees as a
source of his pain. But he will find that the pain follows him
around. Leaving the Church does not make it go away. And
of course, it is not the Church itself or its teachings that are
the problem, but rather the persons who failed to follow the
Church and its teachings. In fact, it was precisely because the
one representing the Church so grievously violated the teachings of the Church that the abuse was perpetrated.

The remedy for such suffering is first of all that the leadership in the Church ask pardon of the abused and administer
a just punishment on the abuser and ensure that he does not
abuse again. The one abused must be assisted to forgive, so that
he be not poisoned by hatred or resentment. Only then can he
be brought back into the life of the Church.

Sexual Sins

Sins of the flesh are another very common evil that especially plagues young people: pornography, masturbation, fornication, adultery, homosexual behavior, and general deviance are rampant in our society, and even glorified. We live in a society that knows very little about sex but pretends to know a lot. It is hard for me to believe that a society in which more than half of marriages end in divorce (not to mention one rife with impermanent, extramarital sexual relationships) can claim any expertise on sex or marriage. Yet our sex-saturated society constantly offers opportunities for young people to explore and experiment without their parents' influence or guidance. If a young person falls into these sins and feels that he is addicted to them with no way out, he can become discouraged and abandon the Faith. In such a case, there is a double danger: the temptation to normalize sinful behavior because the demands of chastity seem too burdensome and the opposite temptation to believe that God refuses to forgive them or help them out of their sins. In fact, the first case is really rooted in despair, and if you can give hope to your child that he can be freed from this sin, he often will give up pretending that his impurity is not a sin.

Just as with bodily health, prevention and early detection are the best medicine for sexual sins. I have already spoken about preventative measures in chapter 6. But sometimes, even with your best efforts, these measures fail. The most effective way to discover if your children have fallen prey to sexual sins is to have a habit of open, ongoing conversation with your children in which you assure them that if they have fallen in this area, you are there to help them, not condemn them. Once they are in their early teens, don't be afraid to ask them periodically if they need help in this area. Your children should feel safe, not frightened that you will reject them and be ashamed of them when they talk with you about sex.

If you discover that your child has fallen prey to these sins and so fallen away from the Faith, it is important to respond in the right way. Do not humiliate your child, heaping shame upon him. He feels humiliated enough, and he needs your help not your anger. Explain to him that you want to help him, and how sad you are that you were not able to protect him. Give him confidence that he can overcome this sin with God's grace and his parents' loving concern. If you are dealing with an adolescent child living at home, you can be more proactive and insistent about changing his behavior and access to near occasions of sin. But if you are dealing with an adult child, especially one who lives outside the home, you should plead or ask him to change, rather than insist.

Sometimes, a child so successfully hides his sins that the parents find out only after the child has been habitually living with them. A young man or woman may move in with a girlfriend or boyfriend and simply announce it to you shamelessly. (Young people rarely recognize that the lives of parents are always intertwined with the lives of their children.) In such cases, when you are taken by surprise, be clear about what is right and wrong. Never compromise in a way that implies that sin will make your children happy or that it may be the right choice "for them" (which is what they will claim).

For example, you must not permit the boyfriend or girlfriend to stay overnight in the same room. Do not visit or give housewarming items to a cohabitating couple as if they were in a real marriage. On the other hand, you should continue to interact with your child in loving ways that do not imply approval of their sinful behavior. Do not be overly scrupulous about how your love and attention may be misused. Instead, be like the father in the parable of the prodigal son. Give your children what they need to live, even if you suspect that they will abuse your gifts. After all, God knows for a fact when we will abuse his gifts, and he still gives them to us as a sign of his love and care. In general, then, the principle is to keep up communication without compromising moral principles.

Homosexual Behavior

Another reason young people fall away from the Faith is that their identification with feelings of same-sex attraction makes it seem impossible for them to continue professing a religion that condemns homosexual behavior.

Recently, there has been a surge in homosexual behavior among young people, largely because it is glorified in public media today. Many children, especially those raised in urban environments without a lot of contact with the natural world, go through a sexually ambiguous stage where they have sexual feelings for persons of either sex. If a child is encouraged to pursue those feelings with someone of the same sex, this can crystalize into more lasting same-sex attraction.[31]

While there is no simple formula for preventing same-sex attraction in your child, there are certain preventative measures someone can take to reduce the risk of a child forming same-sex attraction. Perhaps the most important thing a parent can do is be loving and affectionate toward their children of the same sex (especially during the first few years of life), showing them that you want them to identify with you and

---

31 I do not intend to take a single position on the origins of same-sex attraction. The truth seems to be that there are many causes and some cases are significantly different from others. It is certain that many people made no conscious choice in the matter of sexual attraction. From the first moment they were aware of sexual feelings, these were directed toward someone of the same sex. Of course, that is not the same as "being born that way." No one is born with sexual desires. It is only with the onset of adolescence that a young person becomes conscious of sexual desires. But the fact that someone cannot choose to feel otherwise is no reason to permit this behavior. A man who feels attracted to a woman other than his wife may not be able to change how he feels. The man who has a strong desire for alcohol or drugs may not be able to change how he feels. Yet all of these feelings are contrary to human nature. A natural inclination is one that is necessary for the existence or well-being of human nature. The inclination to breathe, eat, and reproduce are instances of natural inclinations, and even if someone loses the conscious inclination to perform these activities (as when a sick person loses his appetite), it is still necessary that he do what is good for the well-being of his nature.

be with you and like you. You should also be loving and affectionate toward your spouse at the same time, since this will imprint the experience of a healthy conjugal relationship upon their hearts.

Dealing with a child who has same-sex attraction poses special difficulties because of the false narrative being spread in the media about the true character of homosexual desires and actions. The first false narrative about homosexual attraction is that it defines who a person is. Your child will have been bombarded with the propaganda that if your parents don't accept your homosexual behavior, they are rejecting who you *are*.

This is an insidious lie.

Human beings are not defined by their sexual drives but by their creation in the image and likeness of God and by the use of their will to make free choices. The modern narrative about personal identity is really a reductionist, Freudian view that lowers human beings to the status of mere animals. You must affirm this over and over again to your children: they are not just animals, slaves to sense appetites. Human happiness and fulfilment are not found in sex, but in spiritual knowledge and love of God and of other persons. Sex only contributes to our happiness when it is done in a reasonable way that follows the purpose of human nature.

The second false narrative about homosexual attraction is that persons with same-sex attraction are singled out by the Church as "disordered" and are treated as not worthy of God's love. According to the Church, people with heterosexual attraction can get married and live together, the narrative goes, so why can't gay people marry people of the same sex? That the Church prohibits this is proof of its "homophobia."

In reality, the Church does not single out persons with same-sex attraction for their sexual sins. The teaching of the Church is very consistent: every sexual act must be open to the generation of life and must be between persons who are in a lifelong communion ordered to the generation of children.

Heterosexual fornicators, adulterers, and users of contraception are also called to repent and challenged to order their use of sex in a right and natural way. Yes, homosexual acts are intrinsically disordered, meaning that by their nature they do not lead to the fulfilment of human nature or God's law. But the Church also teaches that *every* human person has some kind of disordered inclinations, not just persons with same-sex attraction. This is the dogma of original sin.

The married man who finds women other than his wife attractive cannot simply say, "I was born this way. I can't choose to feel otherwise, so I have a right to sex with women other than my wife." He might even have desires for women other than his wife that are stronger than the desires someone with same-sex attraction has for men. The Church still says to him, "You must be chaste," and calls him to heal and re-order his desires. So all of us are in the same sinking boat of original sin, bailing away. Everyone has to struggle against whatever unreasonable sexual desires they have. Even St. Paul, a great saint, once wrote:

> For I know that good does not dwell in me, that is, in my flesh. The willing is ready at hand, but doing the good is not. For I do not do the good I want, but I do the evil I do not want. Now if I do what I do not want, it is no longer I who do it, but sin that dwells in me. So, then, I discover the principle that when I want to do right, evil is at hand. For I take delight in the law of God, in my inner self, but I see in my members another principle at war with the law of my mind, taking me captive to the law of sin that dwells in my members. Miserable one that I am! Who will deliver me from this mortal body? Thanks be to God through Jesus Christ our Lord. Therefore, I myself, with my mind, serve the law of God but, with my flesh, the law of sin (Rom. 7:18-25 (NAB)).

So the Church teaches that a person is not defined by his disordered inclinations. The married man's identity is not to be an adulterer, and the identity of the person with same-sex attraction is not to be a homosexual. Our identity is to be a child of God, a redeemed child who is loved no matter what we've done, and no matter how we feel. Happiness can only come by acknowledging our identity and dignity as children of God.

The third false narrative about homosexual behavior is that the Church is against true love between persons of the same sex. That is not true. The Church is not against homosexual love, but rather it is against homo-genital sex.[32] Sex and love are not the same thing. Even persons with same-sex attraction can have a healthy friendship with other persons of the same sex.

It often happens that even after a parent has explained these truths to a child, the child still chooses to follow his sexual attractions. All of us know how powerful sexual desires can be, and so it is not surprising when someone chooses to follow them contrary to right reason. In this case, patience is necessary. Pray for your child. Keep the lines of communication open. Don't disown or reject him.

Here, as in other cases, you must distinguish between the way you treat an adolescent child living at home and an adult child, especially one living away from home. With an adolescent child at home you can and should be very directive, even sometimes commanding him not to spend time with certain people or go to places that are likely to reinforce homosexual behavior. With an adult child at home you can be directive, but less so than you would be with an adolescent. With adult

---

32 In fact, even the outward semblance of a conjugal relationship between persons of the same sex would be wrong, even if they were not in fact sexually active. First because it gives the public impression that conjugal love between persons of the same sex is possible. It also fails to appreciate that friendship between persons of the same sex is not the same thing as romantic or conjugal love (even absent genital expression). Thus, for example, romantic gestures of affection between persons of the same sex would also be wrong.

children out of the home, your role is largely to pray and to encourage a return to the moral principles you taught them in their youth.

There are, of course, other considerations pertaining to the common good of the family. If there are other small children in the home who might be corrupted by a bad example, there may be reasons to restrict communication between the younger children and the child who has decided to engage publicly in sinful behavior. And as with other sexually sinful situations, take care that you interact in ways that don't signal approval of the behavior. It's not wrong to meet a child's same-sex partner and treat him with respect. But even though you may feel moved by love (or a desire to show your tolerance) to condone what your child thinks is making him happy, do not do so either in word or deed. If your child was convinced that eating poison would make him happy, you would not condone it. So also, you should not give your approval to things that poison his soul.

What are some concrete steps you can take to help bring your child back to the Faith if he has fallen into a life of sexual promiscuity, whether either homosexual or heterosexual?

First and foremost, you must pray and sacrifice. Only God can move hearts, and prayer and sacrifice are the privileged instruments he uses to give the grace of conversion to souls. Second, the testimony of those who have gone down the road of sexual promiscuity and have returned to the Faith can be very valuable. Groups such as Courage, which ministers to persons with same-sex attraction and helps them to find healing and reintegration into the life of the Church, make good use of such testimonies and witnesses. Third, work on your relationship with your child. Sometimes a parent has deeply wounded his child unknowingly, and healing that wound by asking for and offering forgiveness can go a long way toward curbing disordered sexual desires.

One final caveat: there are movements in the Church today that seek to downplay the seriousness of homosexual actions and even to normalize homosexual behavior (and frankly all disordered sexual behavior). They speak as if it is only a matter of time before the Church "catches up" to society and learns to accept homosexual behavior as a legitimate form of Christian love. Some Catholic parents have been deceived into entrusting their children to persons who promise to help them in this way. Avoid these wolves in sheep's clothing at all costs, since they love the sin but hate the sinner. St. Peter condemns such persons in his second epistle when he writes:

> These are waterless springs and mists driven by a storm; for them the nether gloom of darkness has been reserved. For, uttering loud boasts of folly, they entice with licentious passions of the flesh men who have barely escaped from those who live in error. They promise them freedom, but they themselves are slaves of corruption; for whatever overcomes a man, to that he is enslaved. For if, after they have escaped the defilements of the world through the knowledge of our Lord and Savior Jesus Christ, they are again entangled in them and overpowered, the last state has become worse for them than the first. For it would have been better for them never to have known the way of righteousness than after knowing it to turn back from the holy commandment delivered to them (2 Pet. 2:17-21).

Gender Dysphoria

Another serious problem that has recently become acute[33] for Catholic parents is gender dysphoria, that is, a young person's conviction that his biological sex does not correspond to his

---

33 To cite one striking piece of evidence for this, recently in Great Britain the number of persons seeking hormone treatments to alter their sexual appearance increased by forty-nine times (4,900 percent) within a one-year period.

inner sense of his sex. Apart from driving children away from the Faith, the effects of gender dysphoria can be devastating upon families. Parents describe the experience as equivalent to losing their son or daughter. Just as with homosexual behavior, there are many media-driven false narratives surrounding gender dysphoria that you will encounter if your child suffers from this disorder. And as with homosexual behavior, identifying those false narratives and learning to replace them with the truth is a necessary first step to bringing your child back to the Faith—and leading him to the healing he needs.

The first false narrative is that "gender" is a social construct that is different from biological sex.[34] The word *gender* has not been used that way in the past, so clearly there is an attempt to redefine words in order to indoctrinate people away from the natural truth that a human being's biological sex and gender are integrated. Even so, the attempt to separate gender from biological sex cannot explain why someone with gender dysphoria would want to try to change his biological sex through surgeries and hormones. Indeed, it is precisely *because* people perceive a necessary identification between their gender and their biological sex that some attempt to make their biological sex identical with their perception of their gender.

A second false narrative about gender dysphoria is that parents who do not accept their child's sexual identification are rejecting who they are. The truth is the reverse: persons who deny their own biological sex are rejecting who *they* are. Maleness and femaleness are integral to someone's person. The dogma of the resurrection of the body teaches that each person will be resurrected with his body and will retain his sex at the resurrection. There is no way to "change" sex. A man who

---

34 The philosophy behind gender theories is a kind of dualism that sees the soul and body as different substances that can be mismatched. The Church teaches that soul and body together constitute one substance, and that no one is a "mistake" with a soul mismatched to their body.

undergoes hormone treatments and "reassignment" surgery is
no more a woman than the elephant-shaped bushes at Disneyland are elephants. The man is just a woman-shaped man, right
down to the cellular level. A person who tries to change his sex
is running away from himself and will inevitably be disappointed.[35] This is not an indicator of happiness and fulfilment.

If your child begins to manifest a desire to act like a member of the opposite sex, I recommend educating yourself first.[36]
This will help you to understand the struggles your child is
having and offer some constructive ways to help them.

The next step is to recognize that your child's pain is very
real and intense. Be patient and loving. To the extent that you
can, try to get him good psychiatric assistance. Fortunately, the
great majority of children who manifest signs of gender dysphoria in prepubescent years grow out of those feelings by the
time they reach adolescence. But if your child does not, assure
him that you want to help him come to accept who he is. Assure him that even if he wants to reject himself, you will never
reject him. Tell him that he is not a mistake: God did not make
a mistake in making him or her male or female. He or she will
always be your son or daughter.

All that being said, as with children's sexually sinful lifestyles
there is a line you must not cross in attempting to love and support your child. Do not refer to your child with pronouns of
the opposite sex or change from saying "son" to "daughter" or

---

35 A recent authoritative study on the matter conducted in Sweden indicates
that the suicide rate for those who undergo "reassignment" surgeries is nearly
twenty times the suicide rate of the general population. The results of this study
can be read online at: https://journals.plos.org/plosone/article?id=10.1371/
journal.pone.0016885

36 One helpful book on this topic is: "When Harry Became Sally" by Ryan
T. Anderson. It delves into the history, philosophy, and psychology behind
gender dysphoria. I also recommend reading an article by Joseph Nicolosi in
Crisis magazine entitled "The Traumatic Foundation of Gender Dysphoria"
(Jan. 6, 2020).

"daughter" to "son." Calling a man a woman is a lie and calling a woman a man is a lie. And it can only harm your child and give him the impression that you approve of or share in the false idea that he should and can change his sex. Strictly speaking, there is more leeway if your child wants you to call him by a new proper name, since names in *themselves* do not signify one sex or the other. However, you should resist this as well, since it not only suggests approval but it also constitutes a rejection of your parenthood. It belongs to parents to name their child; we receive our name from our parents as a permanent sign of the fact that our life is derived from another. Trying to divorce themselves from the sources of their existence in this way will not make them happy but leave them unconnected and disoriented. Human beings need to be in determinate relationships with one another in order to have a sense of their identity and belonging.

As with any publicly sinful behavior, if you have young children at home it may be necessary to restrict communication between them and the child who has chosen to embrace gender dysphoria. This is for the sake of the common good of your family and to preserve the innocence of your young children and prevent moral harm to them.

One of the best ways to help a child suffering from gender dysphoria is to immerse him in a natural environment and get him out of the highly artificial environment created by modern technology and culture. Male and female are the most natural of realities, and the inability to appreciate this is often a result of being surrounded by an artificial environment. Getting your children away from the internet, away from televisions and computers, away from the city and immersed in the real, natural world will help them recalibrate their sense of who they are and where they came from.

Another very helpful thing you can do for a child who has already decided to undergo hormonal or surgical altering procedures is to make them aware of the testimonies of the many persons who have regretted these procedures and who have decided to return to their previous way of life. This can give them hope that it is possible to return to a productive life in the body which God gave them.

It sometimes happens that children, influenced by the wicked ideologies promoted in mass media, decide that if their parents will not capitulate to their desires to be called by a new name and referred to as the opposite sex, they will simply cut their parents out of their lives. This can be very painful—even more so for the parents than for the child. And the temptation will be to simply capitulate in order to keep your child in your life. Ask yourself this question: if your child wanted to be treated like a dog or a cat, would you capitulate? If your child wanted to be treated like the king of England, would you capitulate?

We cannot deny reality even in order to stay in a relationship with our children. Such a relationship would be a mirage, a lie. In times like these, we must remember the words of Jesus: "If any one comes to me and does not hate his own father and mother and wife and children and brothers and sisters, yes, and even his own life, he cannot be my disciple" (Luke 14:26). This does not mean that we have emotional hatred for our family or ourselves, but it does mean that nothing can be equated to or compared with our love for Christ, who is the Truth. If our children give us an ultimatum that we must choose between them and Jesus, we must choose Jesus. By choosing Jesus, we make an acceptable sacrifice to God, and that very sacrifice may win the grace of conversion for your wayward child.

When a parent discovers that his child has same-sex attraction or gender dysphoria, it usually prompts a lot of sorrow and soul-searching. Parents can't help but wonder what they did wrong to cause such a devastating wound in their child. It can be helpful to read sound literature on these topics in order to gain insights (I have recommended some reading at the end of the book). But when all is said and done, you cannot change the past. And beating yourself up over imagined or real past failings will not help your children come back to the Faith.

If there is one final piece of concrete advice I can give about helping such children, it is this: *they must return to their family in order to return to the Faith.* You must help them embrace their true identity as your son or daughter, as brother or sister to their siblings, and then, finally, as a son or daughter of God.

Defections to Other Churches or Religions

It sometimes happens that an older child strays from the Catholic faith into other Christian groups or even non-Christian religions, thinking he will find a truer or more profound religious experience there. There may be many causes for this defection: poor catechesis, a lack of zeal in the practice of the Catholic faith in his home, negative associations with the practice of the Catholic faith, or even just having a charismatic friend or teacher who introduces them to a new faith that is logically or emotionally more appealing.

In such an instance, first remind yourself: *I do not love my children only because they are Catholic.* You love them because they are your children, whether or not they share your faith. Certainly, nothing in your Catholic faith teaches you to reject your child if he does not. Rather, it teaches you to continue to show children love, acceptance, and support so that they may someday see that the same God who instituted the family also instituted the Catholic religion.

More often than not, after some time in a new faith, the inclination planted in your child by his baptism will begin to exert itself more and more powerfully. He will begin to realize that the superficial reasons that drew him to another faith are not as satisfying as he had hoped. When he reaches this stage, your child will start to show some openness to the faith of his youth, and your duty is to help them to see its truths anew.

Sometimes a child becomes deeply entrenched into another

religious group (perhaps even an anti-Catholic sect or a cult). In such cases, parents should prepare for a long-term battle. It is important to keep the lines of communication open with your child, but some prudence is called for if that child tries to pull other siblings away from the Catholic Church. You may have to restrict communication between your children who are still young and impressionable and the child who has apostatized.

In the case of anti-Catholic sects, their arguments are almost always against a caricature of the Church, not against the actual, historical Catholic Church. Either that, or they focus inordinately upon the sins of some who are members or ministers of the Church. Such arguments are usually not very persuasive for someone who has lived an authentically Catholic life, who has known and been aided by holy and knowledgeable priests, and who has experienced the benefits of following the teachings of the Church. But for someone who has only practiced his faith superficially, or who has not had a good experience with priests, these arguments can be very convincing.

So the best approach in such cases is to bring these children into contact with the true Church: its true teachings and its faithful ministers. After meeting and interacting with knowledgeable and faithful Catholics, it will become difficult for your child to reconcile the anti-Catholic propaganda they hear with the real lives of Catholics they know. Of course, it goes without saying that your own practice of the Faith needs to improve in order to manifest that, by more fervently practicing your Catholic faith, you have drawn closer to God.

In the event that your child becomes entangled with a cult, your options are often more limited, since one characteristic of cults is that they try to cut off all communication with family members. But to the extent that you are able, you should try to stay in communication with your child. Almost always when someone joins a cult it is because of underlying problems beyond their particular doctrines of the Catholic faith or the doctrines taught by the cult. It can be helpful to consult an expert in cult psychology to get an insight into why your child may have been drawn to a particular cult, and what you can do to help them escape its influence. And, as always, the most important thing to do is pray with unwavering confidence.

Marrying Outside the Church

Marriage outside the Church has become so common and accepted over past decades that many Catholics do not even know that it is a law of the Church that those who are baptized Catholic are obliged to marry within the Catholic Church. Any marriage of a baptized Catholic without the blessing of the Church is invalid, so even if the persons involved think they are married, they are not.[37] This objective state of affairs does not necessarily imply subjective guilt on the part of the persons who attempt marriage outside the Church. There may be cases where they are simply ignorant in good faith. Nevertheless, the fact remains that their marriage is objectively invalid.

When someone raised Catholic (and not formally defected from the Church) marries outside the Church, this is almost always an effect of one of two things: either the person involved did not even know he was obliged to marry in the Church; or he knew but did not consider himself really subject to the Church in this matter. The first is a result of poor catechesis. The second is usually a result of a lack of seriousness in the practice of the Catholic faith. In either case, it is true to say that the Catholic faith has not been central in his life. Often this can lead to them practicing the faith of his spouse, especially if their spouse identifies strongly with another faith.

If your child marries a non-Catholic outside the Church and begins to seriously practice the faith of his spouse, recognize

---

37 Baptized Catholics are able to marry only according to canonical form unless they have received a dispensation. See canon 1108 (and following) of the Code of Canon Law.

that in some respects God may be mysteriously moving him in a way that will prepare him to return to the practice of his own Catholic faith. The fact that he shows seriousness about some faith and the desire he has to live a faith that unites his family are better dispositions than apathy to any faith. God can use those to lead them back to the true faith. So don't lose hope.

Meanwhile, if the opportunity arises to speak privately with your child about the Faith, take it. Let him know what an assistance your Catholic faith is to your own marriage and love for your spouse. If he has specific questions or objections that are too difficult for you, arrange an appointment with a knowledgeable priest. Because only the Catholic faith has the fullness of truth without any error, it will in fact be the best thing for his marriage and family life, and if you witness this in your own marriage and life, your child will gradually be drawn back into his baptismal faith.

Now for the question that everybody asks: "Can I attend the wedding?" although there is no law of the Church against it, still the question remains: is it morally right to attend a ceremony for an invalid marriage? The principle is: if you can't attend without giving the impression that you approve of their entering into an invalid marriage, then you shouldn't attend. And it is hard to imagine a scenario where attendance at such a ceremony would not be interpreted as approval.

I know this is a hard saying, but I suppose that Jesus foresaw situations like this when he said, "Do you think that I have come to give peace on earth? No, I tell you, but rather division; for henceforth in one house there will be five divided, three against two and two against three" (Luke 12:51-52). But if there is any way you can explain to your child that you wouldn't expect him to approve of something contrary to *his* conscience, and so he should extend the same consideration toward you, then perhaps he will understand.

Obviously, the best way to avoid this unhappy situation is to anticipate the possibility and explain forthrightly to your children that you cannot attend an invalid wedding. You tell them this up front, putting the ball in their court. It is not you who are deciding not to attend their wedding, it is they who will have chosen not to invite you by marrying outside the Church.

Regardless of the situation, you ought to keep the lines of communication open and treat your child and their spouse with respect and kindness. It is okay to have them over to your home for dinner and other family events since that's not indicating that you approve of their marriage. You could even have them stay over, if they were willing to stay in separate bedrooms. You may also go over to their home as well, since that does not signify that you approve of their marriage either. Jesus often dined with sinners: how much more should you be willing to dine with your own children who may not fully understand the implications of marrying outside the Church.

Apathy to the Practice of the Faith

One last problem that arises in Catholic families is that one or more of the children simply become apathetic to the practice of the Faith. It is not that they are angry or resentful or want to reject it. They just don't see the point in it: it neither contributes to nor takes away from their happiness. It's just another thing they do because they've always done it. The human heart is so constructed that it must love something as its first love. And so if your children lose interest in the Catholic faith, it is because something else is more important. Perhaps this is money, fame, or prestige. It can also be a result of a sense that at least one of their parents never cared about it. Sometimes in my experience, however, the outward appearance of apathy is actually a cover for a kind of despair over a hidden problem— with pornography or other addictions, for example—that the Faith can't help them.

Whatever the cause, the response of parents should be to

take initiative and share with your children all the ways your faith has contributed to your happiness. Share with them how it has strengthened your love for them and given you strength in difficult times. Don't be afraid to ask personal questions. The very fact that you are taking an interest in their lives will show them that you care about them and will help them want to practice the faith of their parents.

CHAPTER 10

Remember That Your Children Don't Have Amnesia

For some strange reason, parents seem to think that they need to constantly remind their wayward children that they should be practicing their faith. Every family party and holiday, every phone call or conversation, has to have some reference to their failure to live as you taught them to live. The reason is understandable: you are so afraid of the consequences of your children's abandonment of the Faith that you keep returning to it over and over in your mind. And so when your children go on living their lives seemingly without a thought about the faith of their youth, this makes you feel that they just don't remember what you said to them.

But your children don't have amnesia. The truth is that even when you don't say a word, whenever they interact with you they think about the fact that they do not share your faith. For them it is a painful reality. The deeper cause of this pain is their

conviction that unless they share your faith or act as you expect,
you will not love them or accept them. But this conviction of
your children is already a sign that they do not understand
what the Catholic faith teaches. The Catholic faith teaches that
parents should love and accept their children regardless of their
practice of the faith. Just as the believing spouse sanctifies the
unbelieving spouse (see 1 Cor. 7:14), so too the believing *parent
sanctifies the unbelieving child.*

So my recommendation is that if your child departs from
the practice of the Faith either in word or in deed, you should
say something once and then not bring it up again unless he
brings it up. And when you bring it up, say something like this:
"My child, you are living in a way that will ultimately destroy
your happiness. And this breaks my heart, because I can never
stop loving you. My life will always be bound up with your life.
I ask you to repent. But know that whether or not you choose
to repent, I will always love you and will not treat you any
differently than before. But I won't approve of your behavior
either. This is the last time I will bring this up unless you want
to talk about it later."

If you leave it at that, your child will have the freedom to
ponder his choices without fear that he has to choose a certain
way in order to be loved by you and remain in your life. This
will actually accelerate the process by which they feel free to
return to their faith.

Even if you do this, there will be times that your child will
demand that you approve of his religious apathy or sinful behavior. He so identifies himself with his sin that he thinks hating the sin means hating the sinner, so he will think you don't
love him. But even if your child decides to cut you out from his
life because you will not express approval of his behavior, you
must hold firm. If a person were taking a poison that made him
feel, no doctor would tell them, "I approve. Keep doing that. In
fact, I'll write you a prescription." Instead, medical ethics and
indeed true love demand that the doctor refuse to approve of

or assist their actions. In the same way, you must hold strong even in the face of threats that your child will cut you out of his life. Approving of something that will harm your child for the sake of feeling loved or approved by your child is really self-love. You care more about being loved by your child than about loving him for his good. You have made it really all about you.

Often, the deeper reason why your child gives an ultimatum that you approve of his sinful behavior is that he has become convinced that your love for him is conditional. He thinks that getting you to approve of his sin is the way he can know that you love him no matter what. This is why it is so important that you tell him that you always want to be in a relationship with him regardless of what he believes or how he acts. Love has more to do with *being present* to him than with *agreeing* with him.

Your love for your children is not conditional, it is *relational;* that is, it is always in the context of your relationship with God. The truth is that you must love God above all things. You must even love your children for God's sake. For everything good in your child has come as a gift from God. To make a god out of your child is idolatry. And sometimes a parent is faced with a very real Abraham moment: a moment in which you must choose God over your own child. But as with Abraham, God will give you back your child if you stay faithful to him.

C.S. Lewis, in his insightful work *The Great Divorce,* describes a scene in which a mother (Pam) has unwittingly made an idol out of her son (Michael). She does not realize that it is precisely her self-interested love for her son that prevents her from being in a relationship of love with him. Here is part of that dialogue.

"Well. When am I going to be allowed to see him?" [she asked].

"There's no question of being allowed, Pam. As soon as it's possible for him to see you, of course he will. You need to be thickened up a bit."

"How?" said the Ghost [Pam]. The monosyllable was hard and a little threatening.

"I'm afraid the first step is a hard one," said the Spirit [Reginald]. "But after that you'll go on like a house on fire. You will become solid enough for Michael to perceive you when you learn to want someone else besides Michael. I don't say 'more than Michael,' not as a beginning. That will come later. It's only the little germ of a desire for God that we need to start the process."

But the mother turns in on her grief rather than opening her heart to God or even her son:

"Give me my boy. Do you hear? I don't care about all your rules and regulations. I don't believe in a God who keeps mother and son apart. I believe in a God of Love. No one has a right to come between me and my son. Not even God. Tell him that to his face. I want my boy, and I mean to have him. He is mine, do you understand? Mine, mine, mine, for ever and ever."

The fear that can dominate parents' interactions with their child can sometimes result in a desire to control every aspect of the parent–child relationship. This need to control the outcome betrays a kind of self-love and a lack of confidence that God is in control and that he loves your child more than you ever could. A child can sense that he is not being loved freely and for his own sake.

And so it is very important not to turn every interaction with your children into another way of reminding them that they are not living as you want them to. It is also important not to turn your relationship with God into a mere means of fixing your relationship with your children. A mature Christian life is marked by a peaceful trust and surrender, and a recognition that your child's eternal destiny is finally not yours to control. Rather, the part you are to play is to love God and your children freely, without demanding a return. It is precisely this kind of love that will be most powerful in drawing your children back to the Faith that teaches you to love in this way.

CHAPTER 11

Use Your
Unfair Advantage

———————————————————— ✳ ————————

There are times when you feel discouraged as a parent. You think you cannot compete with everything the world has to offer your children. Everything seems to be conspiring to keep your children away from the Faith, leaving no hope. What can your small voice accomplish when it is drowned out by so many louder, more appealing voices?

But through all of this, don't worry. You have an unfair advantage over your children. In fact, it is an insurmountable advantage. *You know that they cannot be happy without the Catholic faith.* The very reason why Jesus came into the world is to bring to the world the joy and peace only he can give. He said, "these things I speak in the world, that they may have my joy fulfilled in themselves" (John 17:13). He also said, "Peace I leave with you; my peace I give to you. Not as the world gives do I give to you" (John 14:27). Jesus, the eternal Word of God, made the hearts of each of your children. And he made those hearts for himself, as St. Augustine said: "You have made us for yourself, and our hearts are restless until they rest in you."[38] So you can be certain that your children are not truly, or at least not fully, happy. Despite all the distractions the world presents, it is only a matter of time before they realize it themselves.

The mother of a friend of mine is a devout Catholic, but without a strong background in her Catholic education. So she doesn't have many responses to marshal against the arguments people give her supporting their un-Christian morality. Instead she simply asks, "So how's that working out for you?" To be more specific, you say something like, "You have all these reasons why making wealth your first priority is okay, why getting divorced and remarried is okay, why fornication is okay, why homosexual sex is okay, why trying to live as a woman when you're a man is okay, and so on and so on. Well, the proof is in the pudding and talk is cheap. Does living that way finally give you what you want?" The happy veneer is just a veneer, a show someone puts on to convince others, and sometimes even themselves, that he really is happy.

So it's only a matter of time before your child has his prodigal son moment: the moment when he realizes he is not on a path to happiness and that something in his life needs to change. Yet that moment is not yet the moment of conversion: it is a moment on the precipice of conversion. Even Judas came to that moment, but he refused to convert. Therefore, your prayers and sacrifices and your welcome forgiveness are necessary in order to bring him from that moment to conversion. So when that moment comes, be ready to welcome him back without a reproach or an "I told you so!" Rather, share with him about how your faith has helped you through difficult times, and how you want to help him through his difficult time. Be like that good shepherd who did not drive the lost sheep back ahead of him with harsh blows and biting words, but rather gently placed it upon his shoulders and joyfully carried it home.

---

38 St. Augustine, *Confessions*, Bk. I.

It may happen that a child who had practiced his Catholic faith lukewarmly actually finds more spiritual satisfaction by fervently practicing in another Christian faith. Many former Catholics in Evangelical groups, for example, exhibit more zeal and love for Jesus than they did before. And to the extent that a child may have become more fervent, and is expressly seeking to be closer to Christ, you should rejoice in that. But that new zeal has limits. A person can never be completely fulfilled outside the Church because of the lack of the objective means of sanctification and instruction (e.g., the sacraments and teaching authority of the Church) that only the Catholic Church can provide. No amount of Christian fellowship, enthusiasm for the Lord, or private Scripture study can substitute for these things.

The truth of the matter is that when God is leading people on the road back to the Faith, he often works through wrong turns that they take. I have personally known a number of people who became fervent Evangelicals after being minimally Catholic yet who ultimately returned to the fullness of the Catholic faith—bringing with them their newfound zeal. So your job as a parent in such a circumstance is to recognize the good that God is doing in their lives. Tell them how glad you are that they are fervent and serious about a relationship with Christ, but then add that it could be even more profound and satisfying if they practiced the Catholic faith and made use of the sacraments with that same fervor. The single most effective means of bringing an Evangelical back to the faith seems to be convincing them of the truth of the Real Presence of Christ in the Eucharist. For someone who fervently longs to be close to Christ, it is nearly impossible to resist the appeal of receiving his body and blood.

There is another unfair advantage you have over your children, one that you may think is actually a disadvantage. *You gave your children life.* It often seems to parents that the last person in the world that your children want to listen to is you. There is something natural about that. A child is trying to form his own identity distinct from his parents. A fruit that stays on the tree eventually rots. It needs to fall upon the ground and grow up to be its own tree. But your influence as a parent runs much deeper than your child's conscious realization. There is always a pull within a child to stay in communion with his parents.

Many times I have counseled a young person concerning one matter or another, only to have that person's parents come to me and ask, "What did you say? He's completely changed!" And after I tell them the advice I gave, they respond with astonishment: "But that's the same thing that I told him and he didn't change!" In reality, the child always wanted to do what his parents said, but he needed to hear it from someone other than his parents so that he could feel like he was making the decision on his own.

Very often, once a child reaches the age where he feels confident that he is his own person and not merely an extension of his parents with a borrowed personality, he returns to the principles his parents taught him. Mark Twain, in his inimitable style, expressed this fact of human nature well when he was said to have quipped, "When I was a boy of seventeen, my father was so ignorant I could hardly stand to have the old man around. But when I got to be twenty-five, I was astonished at how much the old man had learned."[39] Another crucial moment will come when your children have their own children. Once they see firsthand the magnitude and frequency of the sacrifices you made for them, their gratitude and esteem for you will increase dramatically, as will their willingness to take seriously the faith you bequeathed to them.

Of course, a child's journey away from his father's house is sometimes more lasting. I cannot promise a reconciliation even in your lifetime, but I can also testify firsthand to many

---

39 This quote was attributed to Mark Twain by an author named Fred Rindge about five years after Twain died but does not appear in his published works. Perhaps it was something he said but never wrote.

deathbed reversions of wayward children to the faith of their fathers and mothers, the ancient faith of the Church. A child hears the call of his father and mother down through the long years of his life. And that call echoes particularly loudly in the face of death: the death of one's parents and one's own death. This leads us to the topic of the next and final chapter of this book.

CHAPTER 12

Know That God Loves Your Children More Than You Do

※

We tend to think of the relationship between a parent and a child as fundamentally a biological reality, a consequence of the way animals propagate life. But since the revelation of Jesus Christ, the revelation that God is a Father who from all eternity has begotten a Son, we now know that in God's plan the relationship between a parent and a child is fundamentally a *theological* reality. That is, God's fundamental purpose in creating the world so that there would be parents and children in it was to reflect the eternal parenthood of God. St. Paul implies this when he says: "I bow my knees before the Father, from whom every family in heaven and on earth is named" (Eph. 3:14-15).

Because of this, the natural love you bear toward your children, the way in which you identify your very self with them, is a faint yet true reflection of the disposition God the Father has toward his eternally begotten Son, Jesus Christ. And since we have become members of Christ by our baptism, God the Father looks upon us with the same love, the same identification of self, with which he looks at Jesus.

This is not just my opinion, it is the teaching of Jesus: "The glory which thou hast given me I have given to them, that they may be one even as we are one, I in them and thou in me, that they may become perfectly one, so that the world may know that thou hast sent me and hast loved them even as thou hast loved me" (John 17:22-23). Read those words again. God the Father loves you just as he loves Jesus his eternally begotten Son! How can a soul who reads and believes these words ever despair of any good thing? For if God has given us even his only Son, will he not also give to us every good thing besides?

What is the practical consequence of this theological truth? God looks upon your Catholic children as his own sons and daughters. He loves them with the love of a perfect Father, more pure and more intense than your love could ever be. And he loves them with his whole being, infinitely. So he understands your desires for the salvation of your children. He understands your deep pain when they are away from the truth and the life of the Catholic faith. And he wants you to believe that he understands. As Jesus is said to have told St. Catherine of Siena, "Nothing that you do or can do pleases me as much as when you believe that I love you."

Not only does it please God when you believe that he loves you, it pleases him also when you believe that he loves those whom you love: your children. It is God who has planted the love of your children in your heart as a reflection of the love in his heart. St. Faustina records in her Diary that "after Holy Communion today, I spoke at length to the Lord Jesus about people who are special to me. Then I heard these words: My daughter, don't be exerting yourself so much with words. Those whom you love in a special way, I too love in a special way, and for your sake, I shower my graces upon them."

This same truth is found in Scripture. The Gospels record three times when Jesus raised someone from the dead: the daughter of Jairus, the son of the widow of Naim, and the brother of Martha and Mary. Those are all the relationships within an immediate family: father/daughter; mother/son; brother/sister. So Jesus reserved his greatest miracles for the *prayers of family members.* The Lord also saved Abraham's nephew Lot from the punishment of Sodom because of Abraham's prayers. Just as the Lord loved and saved Lot for Abraham's sake, the Lord also loves your children for your sake. Try to put yourself in the Lord's shoes for a moment, and ask: what would you do for your children if you had all the power and wisdom that God has at his disposal? Once Jesus asked Faustina to try this very thing:

> My daughter, imagine that you are the sovereign of all the world and have the power to dispose of all things according to your good pleasure. You have the power to do all the good you want, and suddenly a little child knocks on your door, and trembling and in tears and, trusting in your kindness, asks for a piece of bread lest he die of starvation. What would you do for this child? Answer me, my daughter. And I said, "Jesus, I would give the child all it asked and a thousand times more." And the Lord said to me: "That is how I am treating your soul."[40]

So above all, as you endure the separation of your child, the Lord is asking for trust from you: trust in his love, trust that he loves you more than you love yourself and that he loves your children more than you do.

Sometimes, after coming to this realization, a parent will ask me, "Father, if this is true, does it mean that I should not feel

40 Diary, 229.

pain because my child is away from the Church? Is my sorrow
a sign that I do not trust God enough?"

Some sorrows are compatible with trust in God, even perfect trust. Jesus sorrowed intensely upon the cross, yet his trust
was perfect. If your child were sick, even if you had perfect trust
that God would heal your child, you would still be right to feel
compassion for your child's suffering. Love makes the lover and
beloved one: they rejoice in the same goods and suffer the same
evils. So it is okay to feel sadness that your child is still separated
from God. Even that pain itself is salvific; for God wants to use
that pain that you bear in your heart as an instrument of your
child's salvation. As a saintly bishop once said to St. Monica as
she poured out her sorrows over her wayward son Augustine,
"It is not possible that the child of so many tears should per-
ish!"[41]

That being said, it is also true that some crosses are of our
own making. And by lacking trust that God loves your child,
you can weigh down your heart with the shackles of needless
sufferings. A lesson from the Gospels will help to illustrate this
fact. We read about two people who are obviously being compared to one another. One person is a centurion, a Roman
military leader. He has built a synagogue and he has a child at
home who was gravely ill. He comes to Jesus asking for the
healing of this child. But when Jesus expresses his intention to
come all the way to his home, the centurion replies that he is
unworthy that Jesus should enter under his roof. Moreover, he
expresses complete faith in Jesus' power to heal the child. And
so at that very moment Jesus heals the child, and the centurion,
secure in this faith, goes back to his home confident that Jesus
has done what he asked. When he arrives home, he finds it just
as his faith had believed.

The other person is a man named Jairus, a leader of the local
synagogue. And like the centurion, he too has a child at home

41 Confessions III, 12, 21.

who is gravely ill. He also asks Jesus for the healing of his child, but his faith is not as strong as the centurion's. He needs Jesus to come all the way to his house and lay his hands on the child so that she might get well. He needs to feel Jesus' sensible presence all along the journey. The word of Jesus is not enough for Jairus. Well, on the way back to Jairus's home, his daughter dies. Jairus is disconsolate, but Jesus strengthens his faith and helps him to continue on. And when Jesus gets to the house, he raises the child from the dead.

The good news is that even for those whose faith is imperfect, Jesus ultimately accomplishes what they ask for. But because of his lack of trust, Jairus suffers so much more than the centurion who had perfect trust. If Jairus had only said the words of the centurion to Jesus: "Only say the word and my child will be healed," then Jairus could have gone home secure in the knowledge that his daughter was already well. But because he did not have this perfect faith, he had to endure the suffering of hearing that his daughter had died.

We have the same choice before us. Either we can trust Jesus perfectly, and say to him, "Lord, I believe that you will save my child. I do not need to see it with my own eyes. I will walk in faith and trust back to my heavenly home knowing that when I get there, I will find my child safe and sound." Or we can tell Jesus that we need to see our child's conversion with our own eyes. That we need to feel his presence all along the way. The problem with that lack of trust is that we will only add to our own sufferings that way. And Jesus doesn't want us to suffer on a cross of our own making. He wants us to believe with our whole heart that he can and will save our children.

Some years ago, I experienced an extraordinary manifestation of how God goes to great lengths to save the fallen away children of a sorrowing Catholic parent. I have a friend, let's call her Cindy, whom I have known since I was a teenager. Cindy was raised without any faith, but through the influence of a strong Catholic family we both knew well, she converted to Catholicism. Cindy lived with her grandmother, because her father was out of the picture and her mother had serious mental health problems.

At first, her grandmother was not supportive of Cindy's faith. In fact, at times she seemed anti-Catholic. But when I was in seminary, Cindy came to our abbey to drop off her son at our summer camp. She said to me, "My grandmother is 100 years old now, and her health is failing. Could you please come talk with her about the Catholic faith?" So I said yes and went up to see her.

Cindy's grandmother was having a recurring dream: she was invited to a party but could not attend. So I told very matter-of-factly, "The dream means that you are invited to heaven, but you cannot go because you have not yet been received into the Catholic Church." Then I asked her, "Would you like to be baptized Catholic?" To which she responded: "That would be nice." And that was that. The next day a priest baptized and confirmed her. She then went to Mass once and received Holy Communion, after which she died peacefully.

The story of a 100-year-old woman being received into the Church is inspiring enough, but it gets even more beautiful. The day she was baptized, Cindy's grandmother said to her, "My mother would be so happy." This puzzled Cindy, and she said, "Why would your mother be happy? You weren't raised Catholic and in fact you were anti-Catholic for most of your life."

"Yes, I know," her grandmother responded, "but I never told you: my mother was a Catholic, but my father was a staunch atheist and he forbade her to practice her faith or to raise her children Catholic." So this end-of-life conversion is something even more: the child of a forlorn Catholic mother who came into the Church so many years after she should have and decades after her own sorrowing mother had died. (The story does not end there. I told you about Cindy's mother; it turns out that when she died, a priest was present at her bedside to baptize her, too.)

Cindy also had a brother whom I also knew from my youth. He had lived a very wayward life, but one day I got a call from him asking me to come see him in the hospital. He was about to undergo a very risky surgery, and he didn't want to die without becoming Catholic. So I baptized and confirmed him and gave him Communion. He survived the surgery but died the next year on the feast of Our Lady of Sorrows. When he was nearing death he asked me to offer his funeral Mass, adding: "Make sure it's very Catholic, with Latin and everything!"

Here is a story of a family in which there was seemingly no hope: the story of a poor woman forbidden to practice her Catholic faith and forbidden to pass that faith on to her own children. Yet, when all was said and done, each of the direct descendants of that woman became Catholic by the hand of God who heard the prayers of a sorrowing Catholic mother. It is a story of hope for the hopeless.

Children Are
Worth the Risk

When it comes down to it, happiness and holiness are about acting from love of God and neighbor, not from fear of suffering and failure. By having children, you become that much more like the God of love who took the risk of creating you in his love, and then giving you the freedom to return his love or not. To be happy, you have to take risks. But know that God is with you along the whole journey.

Here is my last word: the best advice I can give you on keeping your kids Catholic or helping them to come back if they have left is to *be fully Catholic yourself*. Being fully Catholic means loving God with your whole heart and trusting that God loves you and those whom you love with his whole heart. It means loving your spouse and your children regardless of their faith or love. It means being a witness to joy and hope in life everlasting.

It is important to remember that God has given us as the first and greatest commandment to love him with our whole mind, heart, soul, and strength, but we sometimes forget that

God has also given himself the commandment to love us with his whole being! It is as if God said to us: "You be concerned about loving me, and I'll take care of loving you. You don't have to worry about taking care of yourself. That's my job." St. Alphonsus de Ligouri says that God loves us so much it is as if he has made his happiness depend upon us, as if we were God to him![42] With such a loving Father, how can we have anything less than perfect confidence for the salvation of our children who are also his children?

When God sent his only Son into the world, he did not send him as a grown man like Adam. He sent him as a child born to a married woman, born into a family. Each member of that family now lives together in heaven, body and soul,[43] the first fruits of our redeemed race. So not only did God raise his Son Jesus up; he also saved the members of his family, and glorified them together with Jesus. This Holy Family knew the sorrows of human families. Joseph and Mary also sought for their lost child in sorrow. Joseph and Mary had to live by faith and hope in God. Just as God loves the Holy Family, God loves your family and wants to save your family. Just as he has made the family his instrument for giving natural life, so too he wills the family to be his instrument for giving supernatural life. Grace builds upon and perfects nature.

If you want your entire family to be saved, then live like the Holy Family. Imitation is the sincerest form of devotion. Pray together, love together, sacrifice and suffer together for a time in this life. If you do these things you will rejoice forever together in heaven. Amen.

----

42 See his Novena to the Sacred Heart, Meditation 3.

43 The Church teaches definitively that both Jesus and Mary are in heaven with their resurrected bodies. But it is also a belief handed on in Catholic Tradition that St. Joseph was assumed bodily into heaven.

Fostering Vocations in Your Children

—————————————————————✳——————

St. Monica prayed tirelessly for the conversion of her son Augustine, hoping against hope for more than a decade that he would return to the Catholic faith. God rewarded her prayers and tears not only with the conversion of her son, but with a religious and priestly vocation for him. Here are her words from her final conversation with St. Augustine at Ostia, shortly before her death:

> What I want here further, and why I am here, I know not, now that my hopes in this world are satisfied. There was indeed one thing for which I wished to tarry a little in this life, and that was that I might see you a Catholic Christian before I died. *My God has exceeded this abundantly, so that I see you despising all earthly felicity, made His servant*—what do I here?" (*Confessions* IX, 10).

God is more generous than we think, and he may have in

mind greater goods for your children than you can imagine. Beyond lifelong conversion and fidelity, God may want to offer your child the gift of a priestly or religious vocation. Therefore, it is fitting to add here a brief reflection on fostering vocations in your children. Yes, we want our kids to stay Catholic, but we also want even more for them—if this is God's will.

A Free Gift from God

I opened this book with a brief reflection upon free will. Keeping your children Catholic, or helping them to return, is not a matter of overriding their freedom or controlling them. Faith is a free gift from God, and that fact is of paramount importance in your interactions with your children concerning matters of faith. The grace of a vocation, whether priestly, religious, or both, is also a free gift from God. In a sense it is even freer, since we are morally bound to assent to the truths of the Faith revealed by Jesus Christ and keep his commandments, but no one is bound to observe the Evangelical counsels,[44] which are at the heart of a priestly or religious vocation. So there is an additional degree of freedom when it comes to a vocational choice. Therefore, be very careful to respect that freedom and pressure your children either to embrace or reject a vocation.

A priestly or religious vocation originates from the very depths of the loving heart of Jesus. It is Christ himself who calls these chosen souls, and he wants their response to be completely free and spontaneous, not tainted with fear or sadness. St. Faustina described a moment when Jesus was calling her to a special consecration to him:

> Jesus made it known to me that, even if I did not give my consent to this, I could still be saved; and he would not lessen his graces, but would still continue to have

---

44 Poverty, chastity, and obedience.

the same intimate relationship with me, so that even if I did not consent to make this sacrifice, God's generosity would not lessen thereby. And the Lord gave me to know that the whole mystery depended on me, on my free consent to the sacrifice given with full use of my faculties. In this free and conscious act lies the whole power and value before his majesty (Diary 135-136).

This is how Jesus wants a soul called by him to respond: with complete freedom in an act of untainted love. He does not want a soul to come to him because of fear that God will punish him, or be disappointed in him, or reject him.

The Essence of a Vocation Consecrated to God

When God calls a soul to be consecrated to him, he desires that such a soul be set apart for him alone. All of us are called to love the Lord our God with all our mind, heart, soul, and strength. But sometimes we love God in this way in part through creatures, and sometimes a soul is called to love God in such a way that he renounces all created goods in order to be able to love God more immediately and securely. When St. Paul warns the married person about being divided (1 Cor. 7:34), he does not mean that the married person does not love God with all his heart: otherwise, marriage would violate the first commandment. What he means is that since the married person is obliged to attend to the needs of his spouse, at times he cannot directly attend to the contemplation and love of God but must love God by way of fulfilling his duties toward his spouse.

The soul consecrated to God is free of these cares that belong to this world. He has chosen the better part, like Mary the sister of Martha. As a consequence, the consecrated soul begins already on earth to live a life that is heavenly. The consecrated soul becomes a witness to the primacy of the life of heaven, to which every Christian is ultimately called. Nowhere is this more evident than in the purely contemplative life of the cloistered nun, who lives solely to unite herself to God in praise and prayer.

How Can a Parent Help Foster a Vocation?

Fostering a vocation does not mean giving your child a vocation. It means making your family and home a place where a vocation can be more easily heard and answered in the event that God gives that call. And the first way to make your home fertile soil for a vocation to grow is to place the Faith at the center of your family life. Unless a child sees that everything in this life is ultimately for the sake of growing in love for God and getting to heaven, it will be difficult for him to understand why anyone would want to devote his entire life to that. But when a child sees his parents focused upon the Faith as the central reality of their lives, he begins to think about how he can do the same himself.

Second, pray often in the secret of your heart to our Lord and his mother to give the gift of a vocation to one or more of your children if it is God's will. Recognize that no parent is worthy to receive this gift, but nevertheless, make this prayer in confidence and full acceptance of God's will, whatever he decides. But don't tell any particular child that you are praying for this for him, lest he mistakenly conclude that you would be disappointed if he did not choose consecrated life.

Third, show great respect for priests and religious, even ones who have problems. If a child sees his parents treating a priest or religious with contempt or ambivalence, he will have a hard time believing that you think this is a privileged form of life that conforms a person more closely to Christ. On the other hand, if a child sees his parents treating a priest or religious with gratitude, affection, and respect, this will impress upon him the importance of consecrated life in the Church.

That is not to say that you should act as if the misdeeds of priests or religious are not wrong. To the contrary, their consecrated state makes their misdeeds even more serious. But when it comes to speaking about any particular priest or religious, you should always emphasize that because of their place in the Church they deserve our prayers and sacrifices more than others. And this is especially true if they have done something wrong. We should speak of the public faults of consecrated persons much in the same way that we would speak about our parent's faults: not with an eye to condemnation, but with a desire to help them.

Fourth, to the extent it is possible, help your family get to know holy and faithful priests and religious. This allows your children to see consecrated life close up, not as some distant, unattainable reality. However, it is important that this be done in settings where your children can see the reality and centrality of the consecrated lives of priests and religious. For example, attending Mass or Vespers at a nearby abbey or convent are good activities to do as a family. And your family's interaction with consecrated persons should not center upon secular activities like going to the beach or a sporting event. Such interactions give the impression to your children that "they are just like us," and that their lives are fundamentally secular in nature. Moreover, such activities draw consecrated persons away from the lives they are supposed to lead.

Last of all, it is important to avoid pressuring your children either to embrace or reject a vocation. Sometimes parents do this unwittingly by saying and doing things that imply to their children that they would be loved more or less depending upon which vocation they chose. For example, a mother should avoid saying things like, "I'll be so disappointed if one of my sons does not become a priest"; or "Pray for my daughter, because I

want her to be a nun." Conversely, avoid saying things that imply that you would be disappointed if your children embraced
a form of consecrated life, such as: "I hope my daughter doesn't
want to be a nun, because I want grandchildren."

When children hear these kinds of things, they may feel as
if they have to choose or reject a vocation because otherwise
their parents will reject them. Then they find out later in life
that the vocation they chose was never theirs, but something
imposed by their parents. Instead, as a parent you should reas-
sure your children by saying something like, "I will be proud of
you whatever vocation you choose; all I ask of you is that you
pray fervently about your vocation and place it in God's hands
before you make your decision."

Remember: God is in charge! He loves you and your
children more than you do. Strive to do his will in all your
thoughts, words, and deeds, and he will reward you and your
family more than you can conceive or imagine. May he be
blessed and praised in all you do.

About the Author

Fr. Sebastian Walshe is a Norbertine canon of the Abbey of St. Michael in the Diocese of Orange, California. After earning a degree in electrical engineering, Fr. Sebastian worked at an intellectual property firm before pursuing further education at Thomas Aquinas College. Graduating in 1994, he continued studies at the Catholic University of America in Washington, D.C., receiving a license in philosophy. Later, while in the seminary, he attended the Pontifical University of St. Thomas at Rome (the Angelicum) where he received a master's degree in sacred theology and a doctorate in philosophy. Since 2006, Fr. Sebastian has been a professor of philosophy in the seminary program at St. Michael's Abbey, where he is the dean of studies.